D0510688

Nationalism: A Very Short Introduction

VERY SHORT INTRODUCTIONS are for anyone wanting a stimulating and accessible way in to a new subject. They are written by experts, and have been published in more than 25 languages worldwide.

The series began in 1995, and now represents a wide variety of topics in history, philosophy, religion, science, and the humanities. Over the next few years it will grow to a library of around 200 volumes – a Very Short Introduction to everything from ancient Egypt and Indian philosophy to conceptual art and cosmology.

Very Short Introductions available now:

THE RUSSIAN REVOLUTION
   S. A. Smith
SCHIZOPHRENIA
   Chris Frith and Eve Johnstone
SCHOPENHAUER
   Christopher Janaway
SHAKESPEARE   Germaine Greer
SIKHISM   Eleanor Nesbitt
SOCIAL AND CULTURAL
   ANTHROPOLOGY
   John Monaghan and
   Peter Just
SOCIALISM   Michael Newman
SOCIOLOGY   Steve Bruce
SOCRATES   C. C. W. Taylor
THE SPANISH CIVIL WAR
   Helen Graham

SPINOZA   Roger Scruton
STUART BRITAIN   John Morrill
TERRORISM
   Charles Townshend
THEOLOGY   David F. Ford
THE HISTORY OF TIME
   Leofranc Holford-Strevens
TRAGEDY   Adrian Poole
THE TUDORS   John Guy
TWENTIETH-CENTURY
   BRITAIN   Kenneth O. Morgan
THE VIKINGS   Julian D. Richards
WITTGENSTEIN   A. C. Grayling
WORLD MUSIC   Philip Bohlman
THE WORLD TRADE
   ORGANIZATION
   Amrita Narlikar

Available soon:

AFRICAN HISTORY
   John Parker and Richard Rathbone
ANGLICANISM   Mark Chapman
THE BRAIN   Michael O'Shea
CHAOS   Leonard Smith
CITIZENSHIP   Richard Bellamy
CONTEMPORARY ART
   Julian Stallabrass
THE CRUSADES
   Christopher Tyerman
THE DEAD SEA SCROLLS
   Timothy Lim
DERRIDA   Simon Glendinning
ECONOMICS   Partha Dasgupta
THE END OF THE WORLD
   Bill McGuire
EXISTENTIALISM   Thomas Flynn
FEMINISM   Margaret Walters
THE FIRST WORLD WAR
   Michael Howard
FOSSILS   Keith Thomson
FUNDAMENTALISM
   Malise Ruthven

HIV/AIDS   Alan Whiteside
HUMAN EVOLUTION
   Bernard Wood
INTERNATIONAL RELATIONS
   Paul Wilkinson
JAZZ   Brian Morton
MANDELA   Tom Lodge
THE MIND   Martin Davies
PERCEPTION   Richard Gregory
PHILOSOPHY OF LAW
   Raymond Wacks
PHILOSOPHY OF RELIGION
   Jack Copeland and
   Diane Proudfoot
PHOTOGRAPHY   Steve Edwards
PSYCHIATRY   Tom Burns
RACISM   Ali Rattansi
THE RAJ   Denis Judd
THE RENAISSANCE
   Jerry Brotton
ROMAN EMPIRE
   Christopher Kelly
ROMANTICISM   Duncan Wu

For more information visit our web site
www.oup.co.uk/vsi/

WITHDRAWN

Steven Grosby

NATIONALISM

A Very Short Introduction

THE CITY OF EDINBURGH COUNCIL	
⊵ 9 NOV 2005	
C0023760435	
Bertrams	21.10.05
JC 311	£6.99
CH	LT4

OXFORD
UNIVERSITY PRESS

EDINBURGH
CITY
LIBRARIES

OXFORD
UNIVERSITY PRESS

Great Clarendon Street, Oxford OX2 6DP

Oxford University Press is a department of the University of Oxford.
It furthers the University's objective of excellence in research, scholarship,
and education by publishing worldwide in

Oxford New York

Auckland Cape Town Dar es Salaam Hong Kong Karachi
Kuala Lumpur Madrid Melbourne Mexico City Nairobi
New Delhi Shanghai Taipei Toronto

With offices in

Argentina Austria Brazil Chile Czech Republic France Greece
Guatemala Hungary Italy Japan Poland Portugal Singapore
South Korea Switzerland Thailand Turkey Ukraine Vietnam

Oxford is a registered trade mark of Oxford University Press
in the UK and in certain other countries

Published in the United States
by Oxford University Press Inc., New York

© Steven Grosby 2005

The moral rights of the author have been asserted

Database right Oxford University Press (maker)

First published as a Very Short Introduction 2005

All rights reserved. No part of this publication may be reproduced,
stored in a retrieval system, or transmitted, in any form or by any means,
without the prior permission in writing of Oxford University Press,
or as expressly permitted by law, or under terms agreed with the appropriate
reprographics rights organizations. Enquiries concerning reproduction
outside the scope of the above should be sent to the Rights Department,
Oxford University Press, at the address above

You must not circulate this book in any other binding or cover
and you must impose this same condition on any acquirer

British Library Cataloguing in Publication Data

Data available

Library of Congress Cataloging in Publication Data

Data available

ISBN 0-19-284098-3

978-0-19-284098-1

1 3 5 7 9 10 8 6 4 2

Typeset by RefineCatch Ltd, Bungay, Suffolk
Printed in Great Britain by
TJ International Ltd., Padstow, Cornwall

Contents

Acknowledgements

Of the many scholars whose work on nations and nationalism has influenced my thinking on these subjects, three merit special mention: John Hutchinson, Anthony Smith, and Edward Shils. From John Hutchinson, I have acquired a greater appreciation for the component of cultural symbolism in the formation of the nation. The important work of Anthony Smith must be the point of departure for anyone wanting to understand nations and nationalism, as Smith has clarified the problems of this entire field of study. Over the years, I have returned again and again to the writings of Edward Shils, understanding better each time his insight that all societies consist of a continual interplay of creativity, discipline, acceptance, and refusal, against a shifting scene of the different pursuits of humanity. I gratefully acknowledge a research fellowship from the Earhart Foundation that afforded me the time to complete this book.

List of illustrations

The publisher and the author apologize for any errors or omissions in the above list. If contacted they will be pleased to rectify these at the earliest opportunity.

Chapter 1
The problem

What is so important about the existence of nations? Throughout history, humans have formed groups of various kinds around criteria that are used to distinguish 'us' from 'them'. One such group is the nation. Many thousands, indeed millions, have died in wars on behalf of their nation, as they did in World Wars I and II during the 20th century, perhaps the cruellest of all centuries. This is one of the reasons why it is so important to understand what a nation is: this tendency of humanity to divide itself into distinct, and often conflicting, groups.

Evidence of humans forming large, territorially distinct societies can be observed from our first written records. Writings from the Sumerian civilization of the area of the Tigris and Euphrates Rivers from approximately 2500 BCE record beliefs that distinguished the 'brothers of the sons of Sumer', those of Sumerian 'seed', from foreigners. During the 16th century BCE, Egyptians thought themselves to be distinct from both the 'Asiatics' to their east and the Nubians to their south.

> **I [the Egyptian Pharaoh Ka-mose] should like to know for what purpose is my strength . . . I sit here [in Thebes] while both an Asiatic and a Nubian have his slice of Egypt . . . A**

> man cannot dwell properly when despoiled by the taxes of
> the savages. I will grapple with him, and rip open his belly.
> My wish is to save Egypt and to smite the Asiatics.
>
> **From a speech of Pharaoh Ka-mose**

In the early Chinese writings from the period of the Warring
States (481–221 BCE) to the Qin and Han Periods (221 BCE to
220 CE), distinctions were drawn between the self-described
superior Chinese and those who were viewed by them to be less
than human aliens, the *Di* and the *Rohn*. In the tenth chapter of
the book of Genesis, there is recognition of territorial and
linguistic divisions of humanity into what the ancient Israelites
called *gôyim*.

> These are the sons of Shem according to their clans and
> languages, in their lands according to their nations (*gôyim*).
> These are the clans of the sons of Noah according to their
> lineage in their nations (*gôyim*).
>
> **Genesis 10:31–32**

In the 5th century BCE, the historian Herodotus asserted a
'common Greekness' among the Hellenes.

> Then there is our common Greekness: we are one in blood
> and one in language; those shrines of the gods belong to us
> [both the Spartans and the Athenians] all in common, and
> the sacrifices in common, and there are our habits, bred of a
> common upbringing.
>
> **Herodotus, *The History***

Plato and Aristotle divided humanity between Hellenes and *bárbaroi*, the barbarian peoples from Asia Minor. The Greek '*bárbaros*' may have its origin as an onomatopoeic designation for the foreign speech of the peoples from Asia Minor that was incomprehensible to the Hellenes. However, in the aftermath of Greek wars with Persia, it acquired a tone of contempt that continues to this day in our use of the term 'barbarian'. Moreover, in his description of the ideal republic, Plato described a familiarity that bound together all those born as Hellenes, as if they were all members of the same familial household. As a consequence, he thought the barbarians were not only foreign to the Hellenes but also their enemies by 'nature'.

> I assert that the Greek stock (*génos*) is, with respect to itself, its own [as if of the same household] and akin; and with respect to the barbarian, foreign and alien. Then when Greeks fight with barbarians and barbarians with Greeks, we'll assert that they are at war and are enemies by nature.
>
> Plato, *The Republic*

Plato used the term *génos* to refer to this familiarity that bound together all those born as Hellenes. What is the character of those societies designated by such terms as the biblical Hebrew *gôy* and the Greek *génos*? These societies have something to do with birth, territory, and being related in some way, a kinship of some kind. Were these ancient societies 'nations'?

Such divisions, where one group differentiates itself from and opposes another, continue at the beginning of the 21st century: both Chechens and Ukrainians consider themselves to be different from Russians; Kurds distinguish themselves from both Iraqis and Turks; the Taiwanese seek an existence separate from mainland China; Slovaks and Czechs have separated, forming distinct national states; Kashmir is considered by some not to be part of India; and so on. The goal of this book is to examine this tendency of humans to separate themselves from one another into those distinct societies that we call nations.

Having recognized this, it must also be acknowledged that human beings exhibit another tendency, when they engage in activities in which it seems not to matter who were their parents, where they where born, or what language they speak. These activities, rather than asserting divisions within humanity, bring people together. For example, scientists are concerned with understanding the physical facts of the universe, such as the nature of light. Light itself is not English, French, or German; and there is no English, French, or German scientific method. There is only science. To speak of a supposedly racial or national scientific method, as when the Nazis insisted that there was an 'Aryan science', is to betray the character of science by introducing considerations that have no place in understanding the physical aspects of the universe. Other notable examples of activities and their corresponding conceptions that bring humans together are the monotheistic religions and commerce. Furthermore, throughout history, empires, such as the Roman and Ottoman, have sought to unify their peoples as a political alternative to nations. Thus, while an individual often understands himself or herself as a member of a particular nation, one may also recognize oneself as a part of humanity.

If a proper examination of the question 'what is a nation?' requires consideration of the tendency of humans to assert distinctions, then it must also take into account those activities that unify humanity. To fail to do so will only result in a misapprehension of the significance of the nation in human affairs; and it is precisely an inquiry into that significance that is the focus of this book. We are concerned, above all, with the question 'what does the existence of nations tell us about human beings?' But what is a nation, and what is nationalism?

Many wrongly use the term 'nationalism' as a synonym for 'nation'. Nationalism refers to a set of beliefs about the nation. Any particular nation will contain differing views about its character; thus, for any nation there will be different and competing beliefs about it that often manifest themselves as political differences. Some may view their nation as standing for individual liberty, while others may be willing to sacrifice that liberty for security. Some may welcome immigrants, and support policies that make it easy for them to become citizens; while others may be hostile to immigration. To take another example, consider disputes today in India. Some members of that nation have a narrow, intolerant view of their country by insisting that it should have only one religion, Hinduism; while others think that there should be freedom of religion such that Muslims, Sikhs, and Christians are rightly members of the nation.

Distinctive of nationalism is the belief that the nation is the only goal worthy of pursuit – an assertion that often leads to the belief that the nation demands unquestioned and uncompromising loyalty. When such a belief about the nation becomes predominant, it can threaten individual liberty. Moreover, nationalism often asserts that other nations are implacable enemies to one's own nation; it injects hatred of what is perceived to be foreign, whether another nation, an immigrant, or a person who may practise another religion or speak a different language. Of course, one need not view one's own nation and its relation to other nations in such a manner.

In contrast to nationalism, the nation is a particular kind of society. But what kind of society is the nation? The answer to this question will be pursued in the next chapter.

However, clarifying further what we mean by the terms 'nation' and 'nationalism', and addressing the other questions raised briefly in this first chapter, involve other related problems: what is a social relation?; what is a territory?; what is kinship?; the appearance of the nation in history; the relation of the nation to religion; and the tendency of humanity to divide itself into different nations. Each of these problems will be taken up in the chapters that follow.

Chapter 2
What is a nation?

> *The nation is a territorial community of nativity.* One is born into a nation. The significance attributed to this biological fact of birth into the historically evolving, territorial structure of the cultural community of the nation is why the nation is one among a number of forms of kinship. It differs from other forms of kinship such as the family because of the centrality of territory. It differs from other territorial societies such as a tribe, city-state, or various 'ethnic groups' not merely by the greater extent of its territory, but also because of its relatively uniform culture that provides stability, that is, continuation over time.

There are a number of complications to this definition of the nation that require careful examination.

Time, memory, and territory

Nations emerge over time as a result of numerous historical processes. As a consequence, it is a pointless undertaking to attempt to locate a precise moment when any particular nation came into existence, as if it were a manufactured product designed by an engineer. Let us examine why this is so. All nations have historical antecedents, whether tribe, city-state, or kingdom. These historically earlier societies are important components in the formation of nations. For example, the English nation emerged out of the historically earlier societies of the Saxons, Angles, and Normans. However, these historical antecedents are never merely just facts, because key to the existence of the nation are memories that are shared among each of those many individuals who are members of the nation about the past of their nation, including about those earlier societies.

There would, for example, have been no nation of ancient Israel had there not been memories about the past, such as the exodus from Egypt, Moses and his bronze snake (which was kept in the Jerusalem Temple until the reign of King Hezekiah (714–686 BCE)), and the reigns of David and Solomon. There would have been no nation of England had there not been memories about the Saxon King Alfred (849–899 CE) and the 'good old law'. Likewise, memories about the Piasts (10th–12th centuries CE) and their kingdom were components in the emergence of Poland as a nation, as were those about the Yamato Kingdom (4th–7th centuries CE), with its worship of the sun goddess Amaterasu at Ise, for the Japanese nation.

The events described by such memories may not be factually accurate: for example, the ten plagues in the ancient Israelite account of the exodus from Egypt, or that the Japanese emperor is a descendant of Amaterasu. Every nation has its own understanding of its distinctive past that is conveyed through stories, myths, and history. Whether historically accurate or not, these memories contribute to the understanding of the present that distinguishes one nation from another. This component of time – when an understanding of the past forms part of the present – is characteristic of the nation and is called 'temporal depth'.

These memories also form a part of the conception that one has

1. The main sanctuary of the Japanese sun goddess Amaterasu at Ise

of oneself. As the mind of the individual develops within various contexts, such as the family or different educational institutions, it seeks out those various and fluctuating traditions that are 'at hand'. The child learns, for example, to speak the language of his or her nation and what it means to be a member of that nation as expressed through its customs and laws. These traditions become incorporated into the individual's understanding of the self. When those traditions that make up part of one's self-conception are shared by other individuals as part of their self-conception, one is then both related to those other individuals, and aware of the relation. The relation itself, for example living in the same geographical area or speaking a common language, is what is meant by the term 'collective consciousness'. This term in no way implies the existence of a group mind or a combination of biological instincts, as if humans were a colony of ants. Rather, it refers to a social relation of each of a number of individuals as a consequence of those individuals participating in the same evolving tradition.

When those individuals not only participate in the same tradition but also understand themselves as being different from those who do not, then there exists a self-designating shared belief, which is called a 'collective self-consciousness', that is, a distinctive culture. Properties or qualities of a tradition are recognized which distinguish it from any other; they are the boundaries of the social relation that allow us to distinguish 'us' from 'them'. To return to our examples, those who accept, and by doing so participate in, the tradition of the Israelite exodus from Egypt distinguish themselves from those who do not. Those who worship the Japanese sun goddess Amaterasu distinguish themselves from those who do not. Those who speak one language understand themselves to be different from those who speak a different language. *The nation is a social relation of collective self-consciousness.*

This distinguishing, shared self-awareness is expressed in and influenced by the everyday conduct of the individuals who make up the social relation of the nation, for example the clothes one wears, the songs one sings, the language one speaks, or the religion one observes. It is sustained by various institutions, such as the Jerusalem Temple for ancient Israel, or the shrine at Ise for Japan, or the Parliament for England, that bear those traditions around which the social relation of the nation is formed. Those institutions provide a structure for the nation. Thus, the nation is formed around shared, self-designating beliefs that have such a structure.

However, the nation is formed around shared traditions that are not merely about a distinctive past, but a spatially situated past. Where there is a spatial focus to the relation between individuals, then place becomes the basis by which to distinguish one person from another. The inhabitants of a location understand themselves to be related to those whose self-understanding contains a reference to that location. The location, thus, is no longer merely an area of space; it has become a space with meaning: a territory. Usually this self-understanding revolves around birth in a territory. One thereby recognizes oneself to be related to those who have also been born in that territory, even if they were born before you. In such a situation, there exists *a territorially formed 'people' that is believed to have existed over time; and this is what is meant by the term 'nation'.* This relation is conveyed by variation of a term that simultaneously refers to both the territory and its population, for example England-English, France-French, Germany-Germans, Canada-Canadians, Kurdistan (literally, 'land of the Kurds')-Kurds, and so forth. This variation implies the following conception: a people has its land, and a land has its people. The nation is a social relation with both temporal depth and bounded territory.

The act of seeking out and laying a claim to a past and its location establishes continuity between that past and its location with the present and its location. This continuity is viewed as justifying the order of the present because it is understood as necessarily containing that past. For example, during the early 20th century, many Jews thought that modern Israel could only be located in the area of the eastern Mediterranean because that was where their past – ancient Israel – had existed. The belief in such a continuity provides an understanding of the self and its place in the world. When one says, 'I am English', one recognizes, perhaps often implicitly, various characteristics about oneself, for example having been born in the territory of England, which makes one English.

However, the characteristics (and the traditions that bear them) that contribute to the self-image of the individual are many and varied. Clearly, not all aspects of the self and the many social relations one forms are about being a member of a nation. If one is a scientist, one understands oneself as participating in a world community of scientists pursuing physical, biological, or mathematical truths. If one is an adherent to a monotheistic world religion such as Christianity or Islam, then one may understand oneself in terms of universal brotherhood. However, central to the existence of the nation is the tendency of humanity to form territorially distinct societies, each of which is formed around its own cultural traditions of continuity. *The nation is a territorial relation of collective self-consciousness of actual and imagined duration.*

The nation, kinship, and community

There are usually other understandings of the nation that support the belief in its continuity. It may be understood as having to do with the eternal, hence continuous, order of the universe, usually as an act of the gods, for example the Sinhalese belief that Sri Lanka is uniquely sanctified as a Buddhist land because of the acts of the Buddha on the island, or that the United States of America embodies the order of God's nature as proclaimed in the Declaration of Independence. Often the continuity of the nation is thought to be a result of a supposed descent from a common ancestor, examples of which are the ancient Israelite belief that the Israelites were descendants of Abraham, the belief that the Japanese are descendants of the first emperor, the Romanian belief that the Romanians are descendants of the ancient Dacians, and, for China, the belief that there is a Han race. Such beliefs in a supposedly common descent are in many cases without factual basis; yet they appear repeatedly throughout history. What accounts for their persistence; and how do such beliefs help us to understand what is a nation?

Humans are preoccupied with vitality; that is, a concern with the generation, transmission, sustenance, and protection of life itself. The obvious social relation formed around this preoccupation is the family. However, the numerous individual families of the nation understand themselves to be just that; thus, the continuation of the nation into the future is understood as entailing the continuation of the families into the future. From everything we know historically and anthropologically about humans, they have always formed not only families, but also larger groups of which families are a part. Parents transmit to their own offspring not only their 'flesh and blood', but also their own cultural inheritance – their language, customs, and so forth – of the larger group, of the nation. This cultural inheritance is usually viewed by the parents as being quite precious to their existence. This inter-generational transmission of one's culture may be part of the reason for the tendency to view the nation as a form of kinship, because what is being transmitted is a part of one's self to one's descendants. However, there is another reason for this tendency.

As discussed, birth within the territory is also recognized to be the criterion for membership in the nation. There is thus a commingling of recognition of two lines of descent: descent in the territory of the nation and descent from parents who are members of the nation. This criterion of birth, and the traceable relations formed as a result, is why the nation is a form of kinship.

> **Kinship refers to recognized traceable lines or relations of biological descent, for example a child is related to his or her parents because the child is recognized as being descended from them through birth. Broader relations of descent are also perceived, resulting in, for example, the acknowledgement of aunts, uncles, and cousins.**

This fact is not to lend credence to beliefs such as that the Germans are descended from ancient Teutonic tribes, or that the Japanese are descended from the emperor, or that there is a Han race. All nations are formed over time out of a combination of different populations, and all nations have immigrants. Although for those immigrants to become members of the nation, they must usually undergo a legal process of 'naturalization'; that is, they must be transformed as if they had been born in the national territory.

This focus on birth places the nation within the continuum of groups of kinship. It is this element of kinship that the prolific scholar of nations and nationalism Anthony Smith has rightly sought to capture in his argument for the existence of what he characterizes as the 'ethnic' element in the nation.

> Similar to the nation, one is born into an ethnic group. Because of this characteristic of birth, both the ethnic group and the nation are often perceived as being 'natural' relations. Despite this perception, both of these forms of kinship incorporate other cultural traditions, such as language and religion, as boundaries of the social relation. While it is sometimes difficult to distinguish clearly an ethnic group from a nation, ethnicity tends to emphasize beliefs in descent from a supposed common ancestor or ancestors, as if the ethnic group were an extended family, while the focus of the nation is territorial descent. Important to realize is that kinship is an ambiguous relation, as it is a consequence of the perception of being related. Usually any nation contains within it numerous ethnic groups.

The nation is a community of kinship, specifically a bounded, territorially extensive, temporally deep community of nativity. The term 'community' refers to a level of self-consciousness of the individual such that one recognizes oneself to be necessarily and continually related to others, as occurs, for example, through birth. The obvious example of a community is the family, where one is always related to other members of the family, irrespective of disagreements between those members. Important for understanding the nation is to recognize that relations that are perceived to enduringly bind one individual to another are possible not only within a family, but also within the territorially extensive, modern nation.

There have been those who have thought, because of these

enduringly binding relations, that the nation designates an idyllic condition of a conflict-free unity. Such a romantic view of the nation can be found in the work of Johann Gottfried von Herder in the 18th century and Johann Gottlieb Fichte in the 19th century. However, no community is free from conflict. Even within the family, there are jealousies and resentments. In the village – often appealed to as a romantic example of a community – there exist many different kinds of attachments as cause for conflict. There are friendships and animosities, groupings distinguished by economic activities and their corresponding interests, for example farmers and traders, and usually competing families.

In contrast to the romantic view of the nation, the actions of the members of the nation involve many different, even contradictory, pursuits. In *The Theory of Moral Sentiments* (1759), Adam Smith caught well these contradictory pursuits when he observed:

> There is many an honest Englishman, who, in his private station, would be more seriously disturbed by the loss of a guinea, then by the national loss of Minorca, who yet, had it been in his power to defend that fortress, would have sacrificed his life a thousand times rather than, through his fault, have let it fall into the hands of the enemy.

The problem is how to account for the combination of sentiments of self-interest and self-sacrifice.

There appear to be a number of incomparable purposes of human conduct, or even areas of understanding to which the concept of usefulness does not apply, for example 'beauty'. Nonetheless, one can still agree with Aristotle that 'every partnership is constituted for the sake of some good' and thus isolate the defining purpose of the nation. However, the isolation of that defining purpose is an abstraction that obscures the unavoidable presence of many different factors in the formation and continued existence of any social relation, such as the pursuit of power over another. Having noted this qualification, the character of the nation revolves around the classificatory distinction of a 'we' in contrast to a 'them' arising from the significance attributed to the circumstances of birth: the relations formed as a consequence of being born in the nation's territory. Thus, that 'we' has attributed to it a relation of kinship that indicates a shared locational preoccupation with the generation and sustenance of life, and its transmission over time.

Patriotism

The preoccupation with vitality involves establishing different kinds of limits or boundaries to respectively different kinds of relations of vitality. Humans draw a distinction between their own children and those of another. One usually does not love another's children as if they were one's own. And one does not usually love another nation as if it were one's own. Such a limitation on the recognition of, and the love for, what is understood to be one's own is a consequence of the preoccupation with the continuation of the self, both its biological and cultural components. The love that one has for one's nation is designated by the term 'patriotism'.

The widely used term 'love' as an expression of the attachments that the individual has to his or her nation is not altogether satisfactory because we also employ the same term to describe the attachments one has to one's paramour, children, friends, and god. Indeed, some individuals have genuinely loved all of humanity. What such a wide use of the term indicates is that, in each of these instances, the individual puts aside, or 'transcends', his or her own self-interest for the sake of others. However, understanding properly the character of such attachments should take into account not only the act of self-transcendence common to all of these attachments, but also the different objects of those attachments. Thus, it may be more helpful to distinguish the love for one's paramour or children from the 'love' for one's nation by understanding patriotism as signifying attachments of loyalty to a territorial community. There are often different aspects to the patriotic attachments that one forms to one's nation, as a consequence of the different factors involved in the historical formation of a particular nation. One may, for example, be loyal to one's nation because of its laws, or its customs, or its religion. There are usually many and differing, even conflicting, views of the nation that correspond to these different factors. However, inescapable is the fact that the individual often shows a preference for his or her fellow nationals.

This preference need not take the form of a prejudice against, or hatred of, those who are not members of one's nation. Patriotism need not deny varying and different pursuits by the members of the nation. It need not reject differing conceptions of the nation held by members of the nation, as nationalism often does. Indeed, in so far as patriotism implies a commitment to the well-being of one's country, it provides the basis for working out the differences, involving reasonable compromise, between the individual members of the nation and their differing conceptions of what the nation should be out of a concern for promoting that well-being. The process of working out these differences through compromise is politics. The concern for the well-being of the nation that includes the willingness to compromise is central to the civility between the members of the nation that makes politics possible.

When one divides the world into two irreconcilable and warring camps – one's own nation in opposition to all other nations – where the latter are viewed as one's implacable enemies, then, in contrast to patriotism, there is the ideology of *nationalism*. Nationalism repudiates civility and the differences that it tolerates by attempting to eliminate all differing views and interests for the sake of one vision of what the nation has been and should be. For example, a French nationalism might consist of the belief that to be a good member of the French nation, one must hate everything English and German; and anyone who does not, isn't 'truly' French.

Nationalism knows no compromise; it seeks to sweep aside the many complications that always are part of life as it actually is. As a systematic, uncompromising, and unrealistic view of the world, the ideology of nationalism is relatively recent, appearing, for example, in the German philosopher Johann Gottlieb Fichte's *Addresses to the German Nation* (1808) and later in the writings of such authors as the German historian Heinrich von Treitschke (1834–96) and the French journalist Charles Maurras (1868–1952). One may perhaps observe anticipations of it in much earlier periods, for example in the Roman Cato the Elder's (234–149 BCE) reported hatred of all things Greek.

The formation of a nation

The relatively greater territorial extent of the nation indicates the search for, and the establishment of, a medium between, on the one hand, the precarious isolation of the tribe or city-state, which can be dominated by a larger society; and, on the other, the imperial rule of empire that apparently inescapably involves bureaucratic despotism. The territorial community of the nation indicates an area of cultural familiarity and loyalty between these two alternatives that allows for self-rule. Its existence implies, as Ernest Renan observed in his essay 'What is a nation?', a coming together over time of previously distinct populations that have much in common; it implies a bounded territorial community of custom and law.

There is thus, as the French sociologist Dominique Schnapper observed, a duality to the nation. On the one hand, there is the appeal to the temporal continuity of a territory and a significance attributed to territorial relations as a consequence of birth, both of which account for the character of the nation as a territorial community of kinship. We may formulate this part of the duality as the acceptance of a limiting tradition that distinguishes one nation from another. On the other hand, there is the uneven coming together of previously distinct localities into a national territory and their respective populations into a nation that is abetted by numerous factors, such as: a developing self-understanding conveyed through history, a law of the land, a common religion, usually a common language, and an authoritative centre with institutions capable of sustaining the nation over time (for example, London as the centre of England with the institution of Parliament). This part of the duality represents innovative, expansive tendencies of human conduct in the sense that previously local customs are supplanted, rarely entirely, by a law of the land, a common culture, and a loyalty – patriotism – to the nation with its national territory. The nation represents an uneasy balance of tradition and innovation.

A nation will territorially encompass a number of different localities. While the spatially smaller village, city, and region continue to exist, they are understood by their inhabitants to be parts of the nation. Thus, the common culture of the nation is only *relative*; it is rarely complete such that the inhabitants of the village, city, and region within the nation cease to recognize themselves as inhabitants of such localities. However, during periods of intense patriotic enthusiasm, such as during a war, the attachments of the inhabitants of the local village, city, or region to the nation may become dominant; but such a situation can only be episodic.

Because the nation exhibits only a relative cultural uniformity, it is often difficult to distinguish it from other territorial societies. It is tempting to avoid this difficulty by formulating categories that are differentiated by degrees of cultural uniformity, thereby distinguishing one form of territorial relation from another. For example, seemingly somewhat amorphous 'ethnic groups' that lack a culturally unifying centre or institutions, such as the Aramaeans of the ancient Near East or the Vandals, Avars, and Picts of the early Middle Ages, and even culturally more cohesive societies, such as the ancient Hellenes or Sumerians, are to be distinguished from the culturally relatively uniform nation. While there is merit to these distinctions, one should resist pursuing them too far because historically the processes involved in the formation of the nation are always complicated, making such distinctions difficult in any particular instance. For example, what is one to make of Great Britain, which contains England, Scotland, Wales, and Northern Ireland? Should Kurdistan or Kashmir or Quebec be designated as regions, ethnic groups, 'proto-nations', or nations?

The complications suggested by these questions indicate that we are dealing with uneven processes of an understanding of the self involved in the always historically complex formation of a shared self-understanding, a collective self-consciousness.

Nonetheless, our use of the term 'nation' implies the continuation over time of a relatively uniform territorial culture. Thus, a number of developments that allow for such a continuation and culture may be ascertained. A nation requires a relatively extensive, bounded territory or an image of such a territory, the existence of which usually involves the following: a self-designating name, a centre (with institutions), a history that both asserts and is expressive of a temporal continuity, and a relatively uniform culture that is often based on a common language, religion, and law. Still, it is more faithful to the historical evidence to realize that each of these characteristics is rarely found to be absolute or complete; rather, they are processes in the development of interests, practices, and institutions, all of which are beset with ambiguities and tensions.

Nation, state, and empire

The recognition by the individual that he or she is a member of a nation is but one among a number of the parts of the image that one has of oneself. Described graphically, it is but one layer of a multi-layered self-consciousness. The layer that represents the recognition of being a part of a territorial kinship may or may not coincide with the recognition that one is a citizen of the political and legal relation of the state.

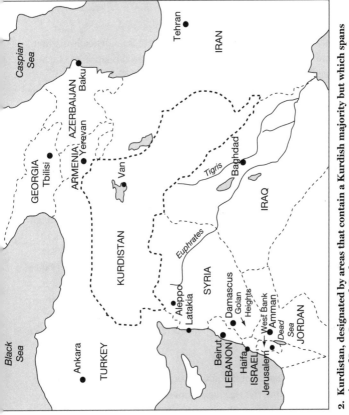

2. Kurdistan, designated by areas that contain a Kurdish majority but which spans sections of Iran, Iraq, and Turkey

> The state may be loosely defined as a structure that, through institutions, exercises sovereignty over a territory using laws that relate the individuals within that territory to one another as members of the state.

The legal and political relation of the state is analytically distinct from the cultural community of the territorial relation of kinship, the nation. For example, the imperial states of the Austro-Hungarian Empire and the Soviet Union contained many different nations. Furthermore, nations have existed in the absence of a state, as did Poland during the 19th century and as does Kurdistan today.

The necessity for distinguishing nation from state does not imply that there does not exist a complex connection between these two forms of social relation. On the one hand, nations have been consolidated through a state's exercise and extension of sovereignty over time; for example, the expansion of what was becoming the French nation during the 12th through 16th centuries from the Capetian Île de France to encompass today the territory of France from the Atlantic Ocean, on its western border, to the Pyrenees, on the southern border, with the northern and eastern borders fluctuating over the years depending upon the outcome of war, the latter being often an important factor in the formation of both a nation and a state.

The consolidation of the nation, in this case of the French nation, does not eclipse the various, at times pronounced, regional attachments. Indeed, it is historically rare for one nation to have a state and for one state to have a nation; many of the world's states are sharply divided by regions that sometimes appear to be 'proto-nations', such as Quebec in Canada or the Basque region in Spain.

3. The regions of France

Nevertheless, the state's exercise of sovereignty entails the
promulgation of law throughout the area being governed, thereby
incorporating various regions into the legal regulation of the state.
Furthermore, the effectiveness of ruling is dependent upon the
standardization of communication, language and script,
throughout the area under the authority of the state. Thus, for
example, certainly one factor in territorially extensive China, with
its diverse regions, becoming 'Chinese' was the standardization
of Chinese script throughout what was becoming China as early as
221 BCE, under the direction of the chancellor Li Ssu. Similarly,
an Armenian script was created around 405 CE.

23

Ա	Ժ	Ճ	Ռ
Բ	Ի	Մ	Ս
Գ	Լ	Յ	Վ
Դ	Խ	Ն	Տ
Ե	Ծ	Շ	Ր
Զ	Կ	Ո	Ց
Է	Հ	Չ	Ի
Ը	Ձ	Պ	Փ
Թ	Ղ	Ջ	Ք

4. The 36 letters of the Armenian alphabet, created by Mesrop Mashtots around 405 CE

Other cultural policies of the ruling centre of the state, such as the adoption of a particular religion and its propagation throughout the area being ruled, have often contributed mightily to the relative cultural uniformity of a territory. This is apparent in Eastern Orthodoxy, a tradition in which each nation has its own saint and church, such as Saint Sava for the Serbian Orthodox Church.

However, the consolidation of a relatively uniform territory and culture of a national community is rarely exclusively the result of a particular policy or set of policies being adopted and propagated by the ruling centre of the state over a formless population. On the contrary, acceptance of such policies often requires an appeal by the ruling centre to pre-existing traditions, whether to language, religion, or legal code. Thus, the particular policy that the ruling centre chooses to propagate is rarely one capriciously chosen as if it were invented out of thin air, even if that policy represents an audacious transformation of a previously existing tradition. For example, in 1501 CE the Safavid Isma'il appealed to the previously existing tradition of Shi'ite Islam to distinguish Persia from the Ottoman Empire, which observed the Sunni form of Islam. The history of the consolidation and stable existence over time of every state reveals this appeal to, and transformation of, previous traditions in the effective exercise of sovereignty over a territory. In other words, the state, although distinct from the nation, generates a territorial community of kinship such that what emerges over time is a national state.

The exception to this phenomenon of the convergence between two forms of human relation, the state and the nation, is the empire, which contains many nations. We may, today, be witnessing the emergence of the empire of the European Union.

There are no culturally obvious limitations to the expansion of an empire. Its boundaries arise often out of military concerns, as, for example, the construction of the Great Wall of China, begun under the direction of General Meng T'ien in 221 BCE; Hadrian's wall as a demarcation of the northwestern boundary of the Roman Empire in Britain; or the defeat of the Muslim forces under the command of Amir 'Abd-al-Rahman by Charles Martel in 732 CE near Tours that checked the expansion of Islam. The protest to this more or less limitless extension of the sovereignty of an empire has been the assertion of cultural distinctiveness and political independence by various national communities of territorial kinship within, or threatened by, an empire, for example the Judaeans, from 66 to 72 CE and again from 132 to 135 CE against the rule of the Roman Empire, and, in the 20th century, India against Great Britain. The explicitly political objection to empire has been that it denies nations the freedom to determine their own affairs, as expressed by the claim to the right of self-determination. However, it may not always be clear exactly the nature of the 'self' that seeks independence, because such a 'self' is in the process of being formed, as is occurring today in Northern Ireland, the Kashmir, Macedonia, and Eastern Turkestan.

The development of cultural distinctiveness through political sovereignty leads us to consider historically the relation between state and nation from the opposite direction: namely, when the nation seeks to become a state. How is this movement from nation to national state to be understood, and, crucially, why does it tend to happen?

The nation seeks a state out of the necessity to protect and preserve the lives of its members; that is, so that the nation, through its representatives and institutions, can act to secure its protection and preservation in the world. If the national state fails to fulfil this purpose (through military defeat or other means), then it risks the possibility of breaking up, because the attachments of the members of the nation to that nation may be withdrawn. New loyalties may then emerge, thereby undermining the existence of the nation. Be that as it may, the determination as to whether the nation forms the state or the state forms the nation is beside the point, as, to varying degrees, depending upon the nation in question, both complicated processes are involved.

The formation of a national state, whether historically a development from state to nation or from nation to state, is burdened with the complications of innumerably different attachments and processes. As was observed, one consequence of these complications is that many national states contain pronounced regional attachments or even other nations. Once again, the territorial relation of the nation is culturally only relatively uniform. Why this is so requires a discussion of the character of the social relation.

Chapter 3
The nation as social relation

Nations are human creations. However, a proper understanding of the nation requires that it be distinguished from other forms of human creation. The nation has the form of a 'social relation'. In order to clarify the character of the social relation and, thus, better understand what a nation is, it will be useful to contrast the social relation with another form of human creation: the tool.

The tool – a hammer, for instance – is a material object whose purpose, as an extension of the hand, is to make human labour more efficient in the shaping of the external world. One can understand the nation as a tool in the organization of life. For example, some evolutionary biologists argue that kinship is a mechanism for establishing an efficient means for an exchange of benefits, because that exchange occurs among individuals who, as fellow kinsmen, trust one another. However, the description of the nation as a tool, whatever its merits, obscures important differences between these two forms. Let us consider another social relation, the custom of greeting between two individuals, in order to distinguish further these two forms, the tool and the social relation, thereby clarifying the character of the nation as an example of the latter.

The social relation

Two individuals, each with their own interests, happen upon one another. These two individuals are merely 'interacting', as they have randomly encountered one another; there is no social relation. However, as one extends his or her hand to the other, these two individuals are no longer interacting. They are now 'participating' in that custom of greeting known as the handshake. There now exists a social relation – the custom of greeting and its performance – between these two individuals. What are the components of this social relation? Firstly, there is the meaning of this custom of greeting. The two individuals in a sense 'find' the meaning of this custom. Where is the meaning located such that it is found? It is located within the consciousness of each of many individuals who recognize and accept the meaning of the handshake as a tradition signifying the acknowledgement between two individuals. Secondly, what is the material out of which the social relation of the custom of the handshake is formed? It is made up of living human beings who make actual the custom by performing it.

The material of the form of the social relation, living human beings, is to be contrasted with that of the tool. The material out of which the tool is formed is inanimate matter. If a hammer is not used, it still remains a tool because it has been established materially out of iron and wood. The tool survives as an object separate from the human beings who live with it. In contrast to the tool, the existence of the social relation of the custom of greeting is dependent upon its performance, which, in turn, requires the recognition and acceptance of the meaning of the handshake. Also, this custom has no separate, material existence distinct from the individuals who participate in, and thereby constitute, the social relation. Thus, the social relation has a dual character: it is at the same time both inter-individual – the two individuals making actual the custom of the greeting – and trans-individual – the meaning of the custom of the handshake in which the two individuals participate by acknowledging that meaning.

As with all social relations, the material out of which the nation is formed are living human beings. In contrast to the tool, the nation does not exist as an object separate from those humans who constitute it. Like the custom of the handshake, where the individuals find the custom of greeting and keep it alive by performing it, the nation is constituted and sustained by individuals who participate in, and by so doing affirm, territorially bounded traditions. These traditions exist primarily in the understanding that each of the many individuals has of himself or herself, for example as having been born in a particular territory. That is why the nation is a form of a shared self-consciousness – a collective self-consciousness, as described in the previous chapter. To be sure, there also exist national institutions of various kinds, for example churches and law courts, which embody, sustain, and propagate those traditions. However, these national institutions are also formed around the continued acceptance and performance of such traditions. The nation has both an inter-individual and a trans-individual structure.

When an individual is born, he or she must fit himself or herself into the already existing nation, which continues to exist when that individual dies. This temporal character of 'already existing' and 'continuing to exist' indicates that the traditions around which the social relation of the nation is formed, for example the national language, are trans-individual; that is, their existence is not dependent upon any one individual, and, in this sense, they are 'objective'. The use of the term 'objective' does not necessarily imply material objects, although the trans-individual traditions of the social relation of the nation may be embodied in and sustained by physical objects such as history books and symbols, monuments and flags.

However, if these traditions are no longer accepted and, thus, not reaffirmed by each generation, then that book of national history or monument or emblem remains merely that and nothing more. For example, the *Annals* of Tilgath-pileser III, King of Assyria

(744–727 BCE), or the *Annals* of the Hittite King Hattusili I (1650–1620 BCE), exist only as objects of interest to historians of the ancient Near East because there is today no Assyrian or Hittite nation. The Roman emblem *SPQR* – an acronym representing 'Senate, People, and Republic' – is of interest only to historians of ancient Rome, or to the visitors of a museum who view the emblem as an artefact of a society that no longer exists. Similarly, the Assyrian, Hittite, and Latin languages, because they are no longer spoken, are 'dead'.

In contrast to these examples, documents such as the American Declaration of Independence, or monuments such as the Lincoln memorial in Washington, DC, or the Arc de Triomphe in Paris, or Buckingham Palace in London, are not 'dead' artefacts of past societies.

They are in a sense 'alive' because the traditions they represent are sustained by continuing to be acknowledged. As these traditions are borne by a state of self-consciousness, they must in each generation be reaffirmed in order for the nation to exist. This dependency on the renewed acknowledgement, however transient and partial, by (some of) the members of the nation indicates that the form and content of the national traditions are susceptible to change. In contrast to the hammer, their form and content are not thoroughly stable or 'fixed'; they are, thus, only relatively objective.

The modification and invention of tradition

Certainly, customs change. They may fade away by not continuing to be acknowledged and performed, or may even be intentionally rejected. Similarly, the trans-individual traditions of the nation and the institutions that embody those traditions undergo change. A nation may transform its tradition of political representation from a monarchy to a constitutional monarchy as the English did. It may even reject altogether such a tradition, as the French did at the end of the 18th century. In this latter instance, since the tradition of the

5. The Arc de Triomphe in Paris

monarchy and the institutions that sustained it were no longer acknowledged, they lost their legitimacy. In political theory, this loss of legitimacy is known as the 'withdrawal of consent'. If this happens, the nation risks breaking up, not because the material of the social relation of the nation, that is, the people, are no longer there, but because the will of each of a number of individuals to continue to understand himself or herself as a member of the nation is no longer there.

The reaffirmation of tradition is never merely a matter of unthinking, changeless repetition, even though those customs that bear national traditions, for example the kind of clothes one wears or the kind of songs one sings, may sometimes be performed in a seemingly thoughtless manner. The reaffirmation of tradition and its transmission from one generation to the next necessarily involves modification to the tradition. Traditions undergo modification because the situation in which the present generation finds itself is always different from that of the previous generation; new problems emerge that elicit corresponding new interests. Often, this unavoidable modification is almost imperceptible, as with the gradual evolution of a language; occasionally, it is a radical transformation, as when revolutions occur. Either way, what it indicates is that no nation can be thoroughly stable as if it were, like a tool, formed out of lifeless material.

Some scholars of nations and nationalism have made much of the fact that traditions undergo modification, drawing attention to examples of various, often radical transformations of how the past is selectively appropriated, such that they speak of the 'invention' of tradition. An example of such an invention is the Scottish tartan kilt. Although preceded by the full-length plaid, which, when belted, left the legs exposed, the kilt was invented in the 18th century. Despite its relatively recent appearance, the kilt has been portrayed as emblematic of the continuity of the ancient culture of the Highlands of Scotland into the present. Likewise, the tartan – cloth distinctively patterned for each Scottish Highland clan – although often assumed to be of considerable antiquity, made its appearance during the early 19th century. Such facts are useful in so far as they clarify that nations (and their customs) are not unitary structures that have always existed. Thus, attempts to read the existence of a united English nation or a Great Britain back into the society of the Celtic King Arthur (early 6th century CE) should obviously be rejected.

However, to concentrate one's attention on the so-called invention of tradition is to ignore the problems posed by the existence of nations in better understanding human conduct. Granted both the occasional invention, and certainly the selective appropriation of the past to serve the concerns of the present (for example, the exploitation by the 17th-century Dutch of Tacitus' history of the Batavian rebellion against Rome in their effort to establish the antiquity and continuity of a Dutch collective self-consciousness), one is still confronted with the tasks of understanding why humans both seek out and radically transform traditions to justify the present, and why those traditions are presented as asserting, or are exploited in the service of establishing, various forms of kinship that distinguish one group from another.

Variation: ethnic and civic nations

As observed in the previous chapter, the flux that is characteristic of all social relations underscores the difficulty in providing precise criteria for the definition of the nation. Even the criteria for membership in a nation, and from one nation to another, undergo over time degrees of modification, for example changing laws of immigration and citizenship. Sometimes membership in the national state is a result of birth to parents who are recognized to be members of the nation, although usually it is a result of birth in what is perceived to be the territory of the nation. The former is often referred to as the 'ethnic' conception of the nation, while the latter is the 'civic' conception of the nation. This distinction may have important political consequences.

The 'civic' criterion of birth in the territory is more likely to facilitate equality before the law, and thus liberty, because all who are born in the territory of the national state are members of the nation and, as such, entitled to citizenship, irrespective of the origin or language or religious beliefs of one's parents. Nevertheless, this contrast between the 'ethnic' and 'civic' conceptions of the nation should not be overdrawn because the historical development of all nations contains a combination of both criteria. Indeed, the criteria for the determination of membership in the nation have usually shifted depending upon whether a nation has been a source for emigration or an object of immigration at any particular point in time. The important point is to recognize that all nations are, to one degree or another, always undergoing change.

This character of only a relative stability – the continuation over time – of the social relation of the nation is not only a consequence of the present generation facing tasks different from those of previous generations. Those traditions that form the conceptual core or centre – the trans-individual, relatively objective, meaning – around which the social relation of the nation is formed are not uniform. There is not only the preoccupation with territorial relations of vitality, kinship; there is also economic exchange; and there are religious beliefs that may exist in tension with both that preoccupation with vitality and trade. For example, there have been times when the well-being of the nation has been thought to require restrictions on free trade through tariffs on imports, as occurred with the mercantilism of the 17th and 18th centuries, and the economic protectionism between World Wars I and II. Religious beliefs have at times been obstacles to economic activity, as when Christianity prohibited the charging of interest on borrowed money. These different traditions with their different interests unevenly come together to form the tension-filled and only relatively stable centre of the nation. The relation between such different traditions within the centre also undergoes change, as one tradition may at any particular time become more important than the others. For example, during a war, an outburst of patriotism may compromise the beliefs of the monotheistic religions in the brotherhood of humanity.

It was observed in the previous chapter that there is a duality to the nation: traditions of kinship that are limiting, and the transformation of these traditions such that they become generalized in the service of creating a more expansive culture. Numerous factors, for example war, religion, and economic exchange, may contribute to this undermining of previously local attachments to village or region in favour of attachments to the territorially larger nation. Another factor is law, promulgated by a recognized, authoritative centre such that there emerges a 'law of the land' that encompasses those localities. Our task here is to examine how law may be a factor in the formation of a territorially extensive nation.

Law and the nation

It should first be acknowledged that the development of written law codes has not always resulted in a territorially extensive, national law of the land. The Islamic Middle East did not develop such a law for much of its history. There instead existed throughout the politically imperial *ummah* (the community of the faithful) various codes of law – Hanafi, Maliki, Shafi'i, Hanbali – each derived from a particular interpretation of Islamic law, the *Shari'ah*. While in any particular region, one law code might be more prevalent than the other three, the Muslim could still choose between them. The simultaneous existence of these different codes of law could only be an obstacle to the formation of the territory of a nation, unified through adherence to an authoritative law of the land. Thus, for much of the history of the Islamic Middle East, loyalties generally gravitated between the village of one's birth and the *ummah*, with various institutions, notably religious orders such as the Sufi, mediating between these two objects of attachment.

Nevertheless, legal innovation did take place in the Islamic Middle East to deal with relations between these two poles, the village and the universal community of the faithful. For example, legal means (the *hiyal*) developed to create business firms and to engage in trade between different localities and regions – means that were not directly provided by Islamic law, the *Shari'ah*. Furthermore, in the Islamic Middle East, territorially extensive solidarities did occasionally emerge, two examples of which were the Iranian and the Berber-dominated Maghrib, especially Morocco. Perhaps the military conflicts between the Turkish Ottomans and the Egyptian Malmuks (1250–1517 CE) also indicate a degree of competition in territorial solidarities within the otherwise universal community of the faithful. Nonetheless, the different law codes that permeated Islamic civilization and the conservative legal principle of *taqlid* (obedience to the Islamic tradition) represented an obstacle to the consolidation of nations, each with its own 'law of the land'.

Of course, other patterns of legal relation are to be observed. In contrast to the impression one gets from many analyses that insist on a sharp historical break between pre-modern and modern societies, there were numerous written law codes throughout antiquity and the Middle Ages. Indeed, as the legal historian R. C. van Caenegem remarked about law in the medieval world, there was, if anything, too much of it, and it was greatly cared for. Medieval Europe produced numerous written legal texts, among them Ranulf Glanvill's *Treatise on the Laws and Customs of England* (1187) and the *Treatise* (1260) by Henry of Bratton (Bracton). The importance of a tradition becoming materially 'embodied', in this case law being written down in a book, is that it increases the likelihood of that tradition becoming stable, hence continuing over time. The physical expression of a tradition can take different forms. For example, languages become stable through written alphabets, as occurred in the ancient Near East, and through the translation of the Bible into different languages: Coptic (4th century CE), Armenian (5th century CE), Old Slavonic (9th century CE), and French (12th century CE). Traditions can take physical shape in the form of buildings, for example the Temple in Jerusalem for ancient Israel and Canterbury Cathedral for medieval England. When this happens, there is a greater likelihood that the social relation formed around that materially embodied tradition will achieve the stability necessary for a national culture to emerge.

A spectrum, albeit abstract, of legal relations contributing to the formation of territorial structures in the European Middle Ages can be observed.

First, there is the canon law of the Church that actually exists beyond this spectrum because its jurisdiction as the law of the believers in Jesus Christ as Lord and Saviour transcends territorial divisions. This is not to deny the inevitable involvement of the medieval Church, as a religious institution, into the affairs of this world, as can clearly be seen, for example, in the Investiture Struggle at the end of the 11th century CE over who, the Pope or the King, had the power to appoint bishops. Nonetheless, I put aside consideration of canon law, except to note its contribution to the tradition of an imperial Europe.

At one end of the spectrum, one finds territorially distinct urban principalities in northern Italy and independent regional states in Germany. While there were developed local codes of law, there was no unifying centre with its own legal institutions, such as an authoritative higher court or legislative body, capable of legally unifying these distinct principalities and states into a nation. In France, on the other hand, after the re-emergence of a strong monarchy in the 13th century, there was indeed a centre, including a royal court and the Parlement of Paris. These and other developments, such as the emergence of a French Catholic Church known as 'Gallicanism', were significant influences on the formation of a territorially extensive French nation. Compared to the urban principalities in northern Italy and the independent German states, one observes the process of the emergence of the nation of France near the end of the 13th century. Nonetheless, the French kingdom remained legally diverse – a condition abetted by the revival, beginning in the 12th century, of the imperial Roman law in southern France in contrast to the north. However, a different pattern of legal relation appears in England as early as the end of the 12th century, so much so that one observes the emergence of a national law of the land.

In contrast to the personal relation between the king and his kinsmen or his retainers, or the personal and legal relation exclusively between the local lord and his vassal characteristic of feudalism, such relations were undermined in medieval England by a more expansive territorial relation established through a law of the land. Some of the legal developments during and subsequent to the reign of Henry II (1133–89) support this observation. There emerged a permanent court of professional judges at the centre (the Curia Regis); and local disputes at the local courts were increasingly adjudicated in accordance with the law of the land by the frequent visits of travelling judges. Also at the local level throughout England, by the time of Henry II, the institution of the jury (initially a body of neighbours summoned by some public official to give up on oath a true answer to some question, but by the early 13th century the means by which to be judged by one's peers) had become the norm, thereby involving the common man in judicial procedures. The result of these and other developments was that the king, as representative of the nation and its laws, and his agents (the travelling judges) were seen as protectors of the property and rights of the individual and the public order, that is the 'king's peace', throughout the land.

Other legal developments supporting the establishment of a territorial relation of the nation include the formation of a national army, as can be seen in King Henry II's edict of 1181, the Assize of Arms, that comprised not only the wealthy man with horse and armour but also the poor 'who need only have bow and arrows'. The call of the poor to the army represented another legal intrusion of the nation into the relation between local lord and tenant. A consequence of this latter legal and military development was to broaden the feeling of responsibility for the country's defence. Common service in war resulted in the awareness that all, the poor and the wealthy, were part of not only their local communities but also their nation. Technological developments also played a role in furthering the attachment of the poor infantrymen to the nation. At the end of the 13th century, the introduction of the powerful, armour-piercing longbow provided the means for a poor foot soldier to be militarily superior to a knight.

Then, in 1215, there was the Magna Carta with its 14th clause, which by 1295 culminated in the institution of a legislating

6. The armour-piercing longbow

parliament, constituted by representatives of the counties and towns throughout England (in contrast to both the Parlement of Paris, which was primarily a court of judicial review, and the French Estates General, which did not meet between 1614 and 1789).

The result of these legal developments was the emergence of the territorial relation of the national community of England, where the king was bound to the law. There were, to be sure, anticipations of such a development in other societies at other times. As the historian Fritz Kern has argued, there was a right to resist the king in German medieval law, and in antiquity there was the apparent subordination of the ancient Israelite king to the law, as suggested by Deuteronomy 17. However, it was in medieval England where these developments were so pronounced.

There were, of course, any number of complications that invited territorial ambiguity—Wales, Scotland, Ireland, and Henry II's claim to Anjou and Normandy in France. There were also other complications in the creation of a national community, for example controversies over religion that resulted in the executions on the orders of the king of Thomas Becket (1170) and Thomas Cranmer (1556), both archbishops of Canterbury; and political conflicts that led to the execution of the Lord Chancellor of England, Thomas More (1535), and the revolution led by Cromwell. Once again, it is the character of the social relation of the nation that it is only relatively stable. What matters here is that there were established both a tradition of public, territorially unifying law – a law of the land – in the collective self-consciousness of the English, and institutions, however occasionally beleaguered, that sustained that tradition.

These legal developments in the history of medieval England represent the emergence of a legal code consistently applied throughout what is, as a result, established: the territorial relation of a nation. Clearly, political factors that are difficult to predict (such as ambitious and able kings who desire to extend their power) influenced this creation of a national body of territorial law. Moreover, legal developments sometimes follow a course of their own that often appears coincidental. The tradition of the 'good old law' in England, conveyed by the English common law ('common' in the sense that it was applicable throughout England), was recognized and reaffirmed, for example, in the Magna Carta. One can only speculate how different the legal and national development in medieval England might have been if the revival of imperial Roman law on the European continent had taken firm hold in England before that tradition of common law was reaffirmed and codified. The point of indulging this speculation is to indicate that many, seemingly accidental factors may contribute to such a development; and, thus, to underscore how misguided it is to insist on one, primary cause for the development of the nation.

The national law of the land expands the social relation in the sense that its consistent application throughout the land results in the fusion of previously culturally distinct populations into a nation. However, this expansion is limited by the other side of the duality characteristic of the nation: kinship, albeit that of a spatially extensive, yet bounded territorial relation. A limitation to the consistent application of the law was one's status – not whether or not one was a noble or a vassal, but whether or not one was English. Beginning in the 13th century and continuing until 1870, no foreigner could hold real property in England, nor did a foreigner have a right to recourse in the local courts. It was thought that land that was understood to be English land was only for the English.

The nation has been defined as a relatively extensive, territorial relation of nativity. We have further formulated the purpose of the nation as a territorially extensive, yet bounded, social relation for the generation, transmission, and sustenance of life. When the nation is a national state, it is also a structure for the protection of life. To be sure, very few social relations, even those whose primary purpose is the existence of life itself, can be adequately understood solely in terms of that purpose. This is so for the nation; and it is so even for the quintessential relation of vitality, the family, which is often a means for the inter-generational transfer of wealth, and of religion. This is merely to recognize, yet again, that human pursuits are varied. The problems that confront human life – how death is faced, how the tensions between men and women are settled, what should be the relation between the individual and his or her society, how human existence in relation to the universe is to be understood – are multi-faceted. These and other problems of life, and the diversity of traditions associated with them, come together uneasily into a conceptually diverse centre, around which respectively different national communities are formed, as each nation works out its own response to these complex problems.

The nation is often described by the metaphor of familial relations and, indeed, has sometimes been considered as some kind of extended family. This is understandable because both the nation and the family are social relations of kinship. Nonetheless, there is an important difference, and to understand this will require a more detailed examination of the relation between territory and kinship.

Chapter 4
Motherland, fatherland, and homeland

Those interested in understanding nations and nationalism must consider the significance of certain words employed widely in everyday speech, specifically, motherland, fatherland, and homeland. Each of these three words is a combination of two terms. The first and second words combine, respectively, the terms 'mother' and 'father', both of which refer to the relational descent of the child from those directly responsible for its biological generation, with the term 'land', which conveys the image of a bounded, yet extensive territory. The third word, 'homeland', combines reference to the familial dwelling and its immediate area in which the infant was conceived, nourished, and came to maturity with that image of a more extensive territory. This combination of terms implies a classificatory category of kinship. However, it is a form of kinship that revolves around the image of a bounded territory.

The idea that these three words share is the concept of one's 'native land'. This is found in all periods of history and throughout all civilizations, ranging from the biblical Hebrew *'ezrach ha 'arets* (native of the land) and the ancient Greek *patrís* to the Latin *patria* (fatherland) and the Arabic *watan* (originally, the village or town of one's birth, and later nation) as in *mahabbat al-watan* (love of the homeland). The appearance of these three words at any particular point in time may or may not indicate the existence of a nation. However, all three refer to the land of one's birth, ranging from village to tribal territory to nation. The continued use of these three words signifies that the image of a definite area of land can be a part of the self-understanding of the individual who, in turn, recognizes himself or herself to be related to those for whom that territory is also a native land. Thus, the category of kinship must be extended to include the classification and evaluation of the self as a consequence of the recognition of not only familial descent, but also descent within a particular territory.

Even the nomadic tribes of the ancient Near East could be territorial. These pastoralists often named their tribes after a particular town or region. Other examples of territorial kinship from the earliest civilizations are societies such as the 'house of the ancestor', where, for example, a city-kingdom was designated as the 'house' of the founder, and the 'ethno-geographic' tribe, the *gayum*, of ancient Mari (18th century BCE). Examples from other civilizations and historical periods are ancient Greek city-states, the medieval English *vill* or township, and the modern nation.

The English word 'nation' is derived from the Latin noun *natio*, which, in turn, is from the Latin verb *nasci* that means 'to be born from' (and from which is also derived the Latin noun *nativus*, 'native'). Thus, the Latin *natio* and *nativus*, as well as the above examples of the biblical Hebrew *'ezrach* (native) and the Arabic *watan*, refer to one's origins; but there is an imprecision as to what is meant by those origins. This imprecision is a consequence of the fact that while familial descent, traced from either the mother or the father, is different from territorial descent, these two forms of kinship are neither mutually exclusive nor historically demarcated. These two lines of descent have, throughout history, overlapped with one another. How is territory a factor in the formation of kinship?

Much of what is implied by this joining together of references to familial descent and territory in the words motherland, fatherland, and homeland is the transmission of a cultural inheritance from one generation to the next that takes place as a result of descent within a territory. Nonetheless, there is a further factual and even biological basis to this metaphorical attribution of motherhood or fatherhood to a territory, because the parental power to generate and transmit life is dependent upon the sustenance that is provided by the land in the form of fruits, produce, and so on. Implicit in this attribution is the recognition that the land itself is a source of life, as Plato observed in his recounting of Aspasia's speech in *The Menexenus* about the physically nourishing 'motherhood of the country'.

> **They are children of the soil, dwelling and living in their own land . . . It is right that we should begin by praising the land which is their mother . . . For as a woman proves her motherhood by giving milk to her young ones, so did this our land prove that she was the mother of men, for in those days she alone and first of all brought forth wheat and barley for human food.**
>
> **Plato, *The Menexenus***

The description of land as mother or father is a recognition of its generative power. To be sure, the expression of this recognition has varied historically and by civilization. In antiquity, it took the form of the acknowledgement of the god or gods of the land. Islamic civilization, on the other hand, has historically been relatively resistant to the development of images of territorially extensive motherlands and fatherlands, especially compared to Judaeo-Christian civilization, in which that recognition has been sustained by the image of the land of ancient Israel as one of milk and honey. Even today, implicit recognition of this power exists, as expressed in the wide use of the words 'motherland' and 'fatherland'.

Home and homeland

This phenomenon of attributing qualities of parentage to an inanimate object (land) can be seen in another example drawn from everyday speech that has a bearing on our understanding of the nation: the distinction between the words 'house' and 'home'. By the word 'house', we generally mean a physical, spatial structure that is not a home, but that has the capacity to become one. By the term 'home', we usually mean that the physical structure of the house has in some way become pervaded by the spirit or power or even moral qualities of its inhabitants. It is as if the house, when it becomes a home, has become a part of the family.

The modern nation is recognized by its members as being more than merely a spatial setting – a house – for the random interaction between individuals. It is viewed as a home, where the 'spirit' of past and current generations has filled up that spatial setting, making it a homeland, a territory. This spirit of past and current generations are those traditions that contribute to organizing an area of space into a territory and that, as such, provide meaning around which the territorial relation is organized. Such territorially specific traditions both structure and provide meaning to the conduct of the participants in that culture. Consider, for instance, that the Sinhalese view their territory as a holy land, Sri Lanka. To take another example, note how President Lyndon B. Johnson described the land of the United States of America as being a partner in covenant, as if it were a person with moral expectations.

They [the Puritans] came here – the exile and the stranger, brave but frightened – to find a place where a man could be his own man. They made a covenant with this land.

> Conceived in justice, written in liberty, bound in union, it
> was meant one day to inspire the hope of all mankind; and it
> binds us still. If we keep its terms, we shall flourish.
>
> Lyndon Baines Johnson, *A Time for Action*

The boundaries of a territory are never merely geographical; they indicate the spatial limit to many of those traditions that are passed from one generation to the next. It was not uncommon, for example, for the territorial boundaries of the ancient Greek city-states to be designated by the respective sanctuaries of their god or gods. Thus, the individuals who dwell within a territory do not merely interact with one another; they participate in territorially bounded traditions that, in turn, influence their conduct: the god or gods they worship or the language they speak or the laws they accept.

These territorially bounded traditions exist over time, having been sustained through various kinds of institutions and practices ranging from patriotic clubs to days of celebration or remembrance that designate events understood to signify the existence of the territorial relation of the nation, for example Independence Day in the United States, Bastille Day in France, the Coronation in England, and Holocaust Remembrance Day in Israel. This cultural inheritance must not be viewed as something external to the individual, like a coat to be put on and taken off. It forms part of the image that you have, not only of yourself, but also of those other individuals who are related to you by virtue of inheriting those territorially bounded traditions.

In the terms of the previous chapter, an image of a territory becomes a conceptual point of reference in the trans-individual meaning of the social relation around which the inter-individual activities are structured. This image is not only spatially expansive; it is also temporally deep. The individual participant in the social relation recognizes as being related not only those in the present who share in those territorial traditions, but also those in the past who performed activities in that territory. For example, even though she lived 400 years ago, Queen Elizabeth I is recognized today as being English. Thus, the territory and its past are recognized as being one's own, as belonging to oneself and to those who are territorially related to oneself.

The possession of both a past and an extensive, yet bounded area of land is key to the nation as a community of territorial descent. Clearly, not all past activities are viewed as being so significant that they become traditions that are continually brought into and, by so doing, contribute to the formation of the meaning of the social relation in the present. However, those traditions, and the institutions that sustain them, that are understood to have contributed to determining one's existence are kept 'alive' by each generation continuing to acknowledge them as being significant. The victory of England over Spain during the reign of Elizabeth I remains signficant because it is recognized that England exists today as a result of that victory. The Holocaust is acknowledged annually in Israel through a day of remembrance because it is recognized that Israel exists today as a home for Jews. Significant past events are often embodied in monuments, as meaningful points of reference in the present, for example the memorial at Yad Vashem in Jerusalem, Israel.

Because it is recognized that one's own life, as an inhabitant of that territory and as a member of the nation, is dependent upon those past activities that have made that territory – your home – possible, a trans-generational, territorially located kinship is formed with references to that past that encompasses those in the present.

The territorial contamination of the blood

This temporally deep, territorial kinship can be seen in the recourse to the idiom 'founding fathers' of the nation. There thus develops a 'territorial contamination of the blood'; that is, an understanding of

7. Memorial at Yad Vashem, Jerusalem, to the millions of Jews murdered in the Nazi death camps

kinship that refers to territorial relation. Such a 'contamination' is the implication of the terms 'motherland', 'fatherland', and 'homeland'; and the very idea of the 'native land'. This metaphorical infusion of biological descent into spatial location is sustained because those inherited territorially bounded traditions are understood as defining part of you. Indeed, in so far as your existence as a member of a nation (and, thus, elements of your self-understanding) is in fact dependent upon those activities of past generations that have secured the land necessary for life, then what is involved in this metaphor is not merely metaphorical!

The human tendency to form attachments to the image of the native land, containing the recognition, however implicit, of the generative power of the earth, suggests something fundamental about human conduct. By the latter, I do not mean to imply that all of human conduct can be understood as an expression of this tendency. Science, international trade, and the world religions signify that there are pursuits that are relatively indifferent to the preoccupation with the native land. I also do not mean to imply that the territorially extensive social relation of the nation is not a human creation that has been made possible by innumerably complicated historical developments, some of which will be examined in the next chapter. However, I do mean to imply the persistence of one among several different preoccupations of the human mind, the expressions of which vary across time and civilization.

There are probably behavioural components to this preoccupation with the native land, entailing various strategies of adaptation to ensure the efficient use and allocation of limited resources in the propagation, transmission, and protection of life that, in turn, are dependent upon control of an area of land and its resources. It is likely that the significance attributed to the attachment to the spatial location of the home also has a behavioural component. The boundaries or spatial limits of the home provide the enclosed structure that is seemingly necessary for familiarity to develop.

Humans seek the familiar because what is familiar is also habitual; and, as such, the structured familiarity of the home provides comfort as it limits the anxiety-provoking multitude of possibilities of action that present themselves for consideration to human beings. In this regard, a parallel can be drawn between the behavioural component in the formation of an animal's spatial habitat and the structured familiarity of the home. However, there is an important difference between the human home and the animal habitat. The human home is not instinctually determined like a beehive for bees, or restricted to a particular environment like the Arctic for polar bears; humans live in many different environments in which they create their homes. Thus, even if there are behavioural components to the human tendency to form spatially bounded structures of familiarity, the very variability of those structures and their locations indicates the intervention of the human imagination in their formation. The role of the imagination in the spatial attachments formed by human beings is clear when those attachments extend to areas that have never been physically experienced by the individual but which are nonetheless considered to be part of his or her home.

This is certainly the case with the territorially extensive homeland of the nation. It, too, is viewed as a home; it, too, is a structure of anxiety-reducing familiarity. As you return to your national homeland from a foreign country, you may experience a feeling of relief. You immerse yourself again in the familiarity of your own language and customs. That is one reason why those familiar patterns of activity – inherited traditions – that structure our conduct and which we call 'culture' are so important to the individual.

Possession

The problem raised by the existence of nations is not only why humans should organize themselves in divisive ways; but also how is it that an individual considers the territorially extensive nation to be his or her *own*. What is involved in the phenomenon of ownership such that the individual considers an extensive area of land and a distant past to be his or her possession, and that, as such, is a factor in kinship? The inheritance of a territorially bounded culture is part of the answer to this question. But there is more to it than that. Perhaps it is the case, as John Locke argued in the *Second Treatise of Government* (1690), that when one fashions or possesses a physical object, that object is considered to be one's own because, through these activities, one has put a part of oneself into it. For Locke, this act of putting one's labour into an object justifies a right to what, as a consequence, Locke thought now becomes one's property. However, our concern with this phenomenon of possession lies in a direction that Locke did not pursue: the consequence of this fashioning such that a physical object is considered to be a part of oneself, and, thus, a factor in the formation of kinship.

When one puts a part of oneself into an object such that the object becomes one's own, and furthermore is considered in some way to be a part of oneself, one's experiences extend into the physical object. This extension of the self into a physical object occurs at two levels. First, there is the actual fashioning of the material object, for example the building of a home or the clearing and cultivation of an area of land. The second level is the contemplation of, including the significance attributed to, that object, so that your memories contain references to that object, even to the extent that the image that you have of yourself is extended to include that physical object.

Clearly, not all objects that are fashioned through a person's efforts, for example the making of a tool, become factors in the formation of kinship. However, those that are integral to life and that are perceived to be so may become such factors. The most obvious example of this process is the relation of the parents to the child. As the child contains a part of the parents, the child is considered by the parents to be an extension of themselves, and, as such, to be their own. This example of one relation of kinship, the family, is relatively straightforward because it deals with the transmission of life itself in the creation of another life. The various forms of this biological extension of the self, ranging, for example, from matrilineal to patrilineal descent, is what is often understood by the category of kinship. Needless to say, complications immediately intrude into this extension because the parents impart to the child not only a biological inheritance but also, as the child matures, a cultural inheritance – their traditions. The incorporation of such traditions into the self-image of the child allows for an extension of kinship as one recognizes a relation with those other human beings who share or have shared in those traditions. This is above all the case when those cultural traditions include a claim to biological ancestry, as is the case in Japanese, Israelite, and Armenian traditions.

The complication in our understanding of kinship posed by the nation is that the object into which one has put a part of oneself and which, as a consequence, one considers one's own, is not another living human being, but the inanimate land. However, land is also viewed as being integral to life, to the life of the individual and to his or her family, where there is a home; and to the larger community of which he or she is a member. When one builds a house, one puts one's labour into a physical object, making it one's own. When one clears the land so that it can bear crops, one makes that land one's own. In both of these instances, through one's activities there occurs an extension of the self into these physical objects; but these are not just any physical objects. They are objects upon which one's own life and the life of one's family are dependent. The home is the location for the generation and transmission of the life of the family; it is also a structure for the protection of that life; and the cultivated land sustains life. This is surely a part of the significance that humans attribute to their own home and its immediate area. These are structures upon which your life and the lives of those who are related to you depend; where aspects of yourself have been imparted to those structures in ways that have not been imparted to other structures; where, as a consequence, there is recognized a spatial differentiation – *spatial limits of significance*.

An obvious limiting factor of significance in human activity is the recognition of lines of descent from the mother or father to the child arising from the preoccupation with the vitality of the self and its extension or transmission. The brute fact is that one prefers one's own offspring to those of another. However, spatial attachments may also be a limiting factor of significance in human activity. Those attachments may certainly indicate a range of familiarity; and, as such, may distinguish the experience of one bounded area from another, revealing spatial variations in the attribution of significance. However, not all areas of familiarity are perceived to be one's own such that they are factors in the formation of kinship. But those areas into which one has imparted oneself such that they are understood to belong to oneself, and that are also understood to be integral to that person's life and its extension, for example one's home, also represent a preoccupation with vitality, albeit now spatially expressed.

These considerations about the spatial attachments to the familial home were intended to contribute to a better understanding of the ways in which the nation, including its extensive territory, is a home, a native land. It is obvious enough that the national territory, like the familial home and its immediate environs, is a structure of familiarity; and that much of this territorial familiarity is instilled into the individual – as a member of the family and as a member of the nation – as he or she develops from infancy to adulthood. Elements of such a familiarity include various customs, ranging from the kind of food one eats to the kind of clothes one wears, to the language one speaks, and to the law of the land which, as such, organizes the land into a legally uniform territory. The bearing of law on the attachment to the land as one's own can be pronounced, as in the change in the law of the early European Middle Ages that allowed the family of the vassal or tenant to inherit the fief (landed property), thereby providing a more secure future for their descendants. Furthermore, the attachment to an inherited fief as one's own and the attachment to the national homeland as one's own can be intermingled when there is a law of the land, enforced by the national centre (the royal courts), that protects the inheritance, thereby encouraging a loyalty – patriotism – to the national state.

There are similarities and differences to be observed between the attachments to one's familial home and those to one's national homeland. While in both instances, part of the self has been put into these respective spatial structures that are perceived to be locational frameworks for the generation and transmission of life, for the family, the primary focus is the parents; but for the nation, it is the territory. For the family, there are indeed significant spatial attachments, as can be seen in the importance of the home to the family; indeed, the walls of the home shelter and protect the lives of the members of the family from external threats. In certain historical periods and among certain strata of the population, spatial attachments to the familial home can be quite pronounced, as when, for example, a family has lived in the same house or town for generations and when one's parents are buried in the immediate area of the home. In the latter case, part of oneself – those who have imparted life to you – has literally been put into the inanimate land. Nevertheless, however important spatial attachments may become for the family, they are of secondary significance when compared to the recognition of the parents as the source of life in the structure of the family as a form of kinship.

For the nation, while there are also attachments to ancestry, they are to those who are perceived as preceding you, often generations ago, in the territory of the nation and who are further perceived as having made possible the existence of the territory as a homeland that sustains the life of the current generation. They are the ones who cleared and cultivated the land, who built towns and cities and transportation systems joining them to one another, and who defended that land in the past. In the formation of the national homeland, those who put part of themselves into the land, making it a territory, are related to you to the extent that you are descended from them by virtue of dwelling in the historically evolved territory which those perceived territorial ancestors created and defended. In this case, the part of the self that has been put into the homeland by those who preceded you long ago is conveyed by those inherited traditions that you recognize as in some measure defining yourself. Characteristic of the nation is the prominence of this recognized territorially bounded kinship at the expense of a territorially expansive, universalizing vision of a civilized life that is found with empires, for example that of the Roman Empire when, after the edict of Caracalla (213 CE), citizenship was granted to many of the residents of the Empire.

The element of temporal depth in the territorial relation of a national homeland, whereby a part of yourself was put into the homeland by your perceived territorial ancestors, is expressed in the significance you attribute to those previous events and those responsible for them in the creation of their and your territory that sustained their lives and sustains your life. There is thus asserted a temporal and territorial continuum between your own society and those previous societies, and a recognized kinship between the current members of the nation and the members of those earlier societies. It may factually very well be that those recognized territorial ancestors and their societies differed in many important ways from the current generation and its society. Many of the customs and laws of those territorial ancestors may have been different; their religion may have been different; and certainly the territorial scope of their societies may have been different. Those perceived territorial ancestors might even not have understood themselves as members of the nation of which you are a member. A necessary factor in the formation of a territorial ancestry is, as Ernest Renan remarked more than one hundred years ago, 'to get one's history wrong'. What does this 'getting one's history wrong' mean for understanding nationality? What is the relation of the nation to history, and how is one to evaluate its appearance in history? These are the problems of the next chapter.

Chapter 5
The nation in history

Examinations of the nation in history often begin with England in the 16th and 17th centuries or the United States and France in the 18th century. The nation is, thus, judged to be relatively recent, to have taken shape as a consequence of democratic conceptions of political participation, the social mobility of industrial capitalism, and technological advancements in transportation and communication. There is much to recommend such a conclusion.

Certainly, the democratic conception of citizenship, an extensive market for manufactured goods and services, and advances in communication have all contributed to moulding previously distinct localities and their respective populations into a national community. Democracy promotes a belief in the equality of the members of the nation, thereby contributing mightily to the sense of the nation as a community. An extensive market for manufactured goods and services, and the advances in transportation that this requires, would do the same through fostering a sociological mobility of the population necessary for the developed division of labour of a modern economy. Individuals leave the countryside seeking jobs and education; they come together in the large cities of the nation. Universities and professional schools are established to educate and train these individuals – an education that includes the history of the nation. Clearly, advances in the forms of communication over the past four centuries (printed books, newspapers, radio, television, the telephone, and films) have resulted in the creation of literate populations. They have stabilized the previously oral culture and its language through print. They have further dispersed that language throughout the nation's territory, thereby promoting a national culture. A territorially bounded linguistic community is consolidated, as language becomes a 'marker' of membership in the nation. All these factors contribute to the definition of the self in the collective self-consciousness of the nation.

However, these analyses proceed by selecting only that evidence that appears to confirm the judgement that nations are historically novel. To proceed in this way and, thus, to reach this conclusion is to disregard earlier developments such as the emergence of a national law of the land in medieval England, as discussed briefly in Chapter 3. This is no way to proceed, as that evidence which complicates the understanding of the nation in history should be acknowledged.

It is often observed that the historical expression of the nation is extraordinarily varied; and so it is. It differs over time for any particular nation, for example the contested views over what the nation is and should be (and, thus, what the nation was) in the American Civil War. It also differs widely from one nation to another, for example from the linguistically diverse Switzerland in contrast to England. The appearance of the nation and its continuation over time is not an historically uniform process that can be attributed to one cause, such as the requirements of industrial capitalism, or confined to one period of time, such as the last several centuries. Let us proceed by beginning with a brief examination of some of the evidence that complicates the understanding of the nation in history, with reference to four societies from different periods and different civilizations: Sri Lanka from the reign of King Dutthagāmani through the early Anurāhapuri period (161 BCE to 718 CE); ancient Israel before 586 BCE; late 7th- to 9th-century CE Japan, encompassing the

Nara Period; and medieval Poland, in particular the 14th century CE.

Pre-modern nations?

An important component in the formation of the Sinhalese territorial relation was the belief, found in the Sinhalese histories of the 4th and 5th centuries CE, the Dīpavamsa and especially the Mahāvamsa, that the Buddha, as a consequence of having supposedly visited Sri Lanka three times and having freed it of its original supernatural and evil inhabitants, the Yakkhas, had sanctified the entire island, thereby transforming it into a Buddhist territory. There was thus asserted a territorial relation between being Sinhalese and Buddhism that was thought to be based on the order of the universe, that is, the actions of the Buddha. Today, as a confirmation of the Buddha's past and current presence in Sri Lanka, there are shrines throughout the island: at Mahiyangana, where the collarbone of the Buddha is kept; at Mount Samantakuta, where the Buddha's fossilized footprint can be seen; and the most important at Kandy, containing the relic of the Buddha's tooth.

In the second example, among the traditions of the ancient Israelites, one finds the belief that Canaan, the land of milk and honey, might not have become their possession because it was occupied by the giant, mythological Nephilim, the Anakites (Numbers 13:32–33; Genesis 6:4). However, Moses assures the Israelites that the entire land will be their possession because Yahweh will lead them into battle (Deuteronomy 1:28–30; 9:2–3), thereby fulfilling their god's promise to Israel's supposed ancestor, Abraham.

In the third example, the early 8th-century CE Japanese Chronicles, the Kojiki and the Nihon Shoki, assert that the emperor was descended from the sun goddess Amaterasu and that, further, Japan was created by the parents of the sun goddess.

Finally, the early 13th century CE Polish chronicle by Wincenty recounts the story about how the body of Bishop Stanisław, having been dismembered and scattered throughout what was viewed as the territory of Poland, miraculously grew together, just as the nation, once its territory was unified, would be resurrected.

In all of these examples, one observes myths contributing to the formation of the image of a bounded, territorial relation of temporal duration. These myths, that is, beliefs with no empirical foundation, accomplish this by formulating, in different ways, a connection between historically actual societies to a perceived order of the universe (the act of the gods). By so doing, the uniqueness of a territorial community is justified, thereby distinguishing it from other territorial relations, for example ancient Israel from Egypt, or Poland from Germany. As we shall see, these kinds of beliefs are by no means confined to societies of the distant past; they are found in the formation of modern nations as well. One thus observes in the formation of nations throughout history what the historian Delmer Brown described as making myths more historical and making actual events more mythical.

It is through history – broadly understood here also to include myths that, as such, blur the distinction between fact and meaningful fancy – that a nation understands itself, and, by so doing, constitutes itself. However, this self-understanding is never free from ambiguity. Why? There are always problems in the present when national histories are composed that complicate that self-understanding. In response to those problems, national histories usually convey a goal for the future by often appealing to some understanding of the past in support of that goal. The histories of Sri Lanka, ancient Israel, Japan, and medieval Poland convey, in varying ways, such a goal.

The early Sinhalese histories also recount how the Buddhist warrior-king Dutthagāmani (161–137 BCE) led Buddhist monks to conquer the Hindu Tamils, thereby establishing a Buddhist territorial order throughout the island. It thus becomes clear that the mythological account of the Yakkhas, earlier subdued by the Buddha, was intended to legitimate Dutthagāmani's subsequent historical defeat of the Tamils, thereby further justifying the sovereignty of the Buddhist king throughout what those early histories describe as a territorially and religiously uniform island. However, the situation 500 years later, when those histories were composed, was more complicated than this combination of mythological and historical accounts of a religiously infused territorial kinship in the service of consolidating power might suggest. The ideal of a unified island, represented by the earlier military victories of the Buddhist King Dutthagāmani represented a goal to be achieved, as it stood in contrast to long periods of instability and regional conflicts during much of the early Anurādhapura period of Sinhalese history (137 BCE to 718 CE) between the southern part of the island, Rohana, and the central kingdom of Anurādhapura. This instability was further aggravated by the threat of foreign invasion from southern India as a result of Hindu resurgence.

For ancient Israel, the image of a legally and religiously unified territorial relation of 'all Israel' was justified by an appeal to past mythical and historical events, respectively the exodus from Egypt and the war with the Philistines. However, this image also represented a goal to be achieved, given the events during which much of the Hebrew Bible was likely written, specifically the Assyrian subjugation of the northern kingdom of Israel (722 BCE) and the Babylonian destruction of Jerusalem (586 BCE). The Polish account of the resurrection of the dismembered body of Stanisław also served such a purpose. The dispersal of parts of the body was a symbol for the division of the Piast Kingdom during the late 12th and early 13th centuries, when parts of the country were under the control of the Teutonic Knights and the Czechs. The body's resurrection would signify the re-emergence of the territory of the Piast Kingdom as the Polish nation.

While these histories exhibit a selective appeal to only aspects of the past to promote a particular understanding of the present and a goal for the future, they still convey complications for that understanding. For example, Tamils and Tamil territory, including for several centuries a Tamil kingdom, have always existed throughout the history of the island of Sri Lanka in ways that indicate an intermingling of Tamils, Sinhalese, and their respective religious traditions. A careful reading of the Hebrew Bible reveals not only two traditions of the occupation of the 'promised land' but also differing understandings of its boundaries. There was an idealized portrayal of the Israelites under the command of Joshua occupying the entire land, whose territorially vague boundaries are from the Mediterranean Sea to the Euphrates (Deuteronomy 11:24; Joshua 1:2–4); and a presumably factually more accurate account (Judges 1) indicating a gradual occupation (by a population that should perhaps be characterized as 'proto-Israelite', for example the Calebites) of the land, whose precise boundaries designate a more limited territory (for example, Numbers 34:1–10).

Not only do the demands of the present force reinterpretations of the self-understanding of the territorial relation, but so do the tensions among the different traditions that are to be found within any nation. In the example of the Buddhist warrior-king Dutthagāmani, the account of his slaughter of the Tamils violates Buddhist principles of non-violence, thereby undermining the Buddhist concept of salvation. Here, the tension between politics and religion is evident. Attempts are often made to minimize such inconsistencies between religious doctrine and politics; for example, in the Mahāvamsa, the Tamils are unethically described as being less-than-human animals.

In the tradition of ancient Israel, there was the belief that Israel was a people uniquely chosen by Yahweh to dwell in a land promised to them by Yahweh. That choice was embodied in the idea of the covenant and manifested, in a combination of myth and history, in the account of the Exodus. Obviously the tradition of being a 'chosen people' sustained the self-understanding of the nation of Israel as being distinct from other nations. Nevertheless, the necessity for modifying that self-understanding arose when God's 'chosen people' suffered military defeat and foreign occupation by first the Assyrians and then the Babylonians. Thus, in the Book of Amos, it is asserted that Israel is to be held accountable to universal standards (Amos 3:2), so much so that its historically unique relation to Yahweh is qualified: 'Are not you Israelites the same to me as the Ethiopians', declares Yahweh, 'Did I not bring Israel up from Egypt, the Philistines from Crete and the Arameans from Kir?' (Amos 9:7).

There is nothing necessarily pre-modern about the existence of tensions within a particular tradition, among the different traditions that form a nation, and how those traditions are used to understand the present. Such tensions are unavoidable because: 1) they arise out of different human pursuits, such as religion, politics, economics, and a preoccupation with vitality manifested in kinship; and 2) the appearance of new problems and demands. For example, during the last 25 years, the self-understanding of the French-speaking people of Quebec has been in flux, as they consider whether or not they are Canadians. During this period, one set of traditions is emphasized over another; different histories are written, some emphasizing connections to France while others do not. Certainly, the tension between religion and politics exists for modern nations, for example in the extent to which the Polish nation is understood as being necessarily Roman Catholic or India as necessarily Hindu.

The problem is whether or not the societies of early Sri Lanka, ancient Israel, Japan of the 8th century CE, medieval Poland of the 14th and 15th centuries as well as others, such as Korea beginning with the Koryŏ era (10th–14th centuries CE), should be considered nations. The answer to this question will determine how one is to understand when the nation appeared in history. In each of these pre-modern societies, one observes expressions of a community of territorial kinship. There is a self-understanding, a collective self-consciousness, which is spatially oriented, territorially bounded, and temporally deep, as conveyed by the very existence of the respective, written histories of each of these pre-modern societies.

Objections

While some scholars acknowledge these historical expressions of a territorial relation of kinship, there has generally been a reluctance to characterize such societies as nations. The primary objection to doing so is the insistence that the vast majority of the populations of these pre-modern societies could not have participated in a common culture. It is argued that the culture of these pre-modern societies was fragmented both vertically and horizontally: vertically, because of the vast distinction between the educated and the illiterate; and horizontally, because the attachments among the illiterate differed significantly from one locality to another. Thus, these societies, it is further argued, exhibited sharp cultural and (because of the absence of modern conceptions of political participation through democratic citizenship) political distinctions between the ruling centre and these culturally isolated localities, the periphery. Because of these distinctions, it is concluded that these pre-modern societies were not national communities. It is thus insisted that the territorial community of the nation must be based upon the development of such culturally unifying factors as modern means of communication, public education, a uniform and territorially pervasive law, and democratic citizenship.

As was observed, there is a degree of merit to this argument. The nation is likely to exhibit a greater cultural cohesiveness and stability given these modern developments. Our use of the term 'nation' appears to imply such a cohesiveness and stability that distinguish nations from seemingly more amorphous pre-modern societies such as the Aramaeans of the ancient Near East and the

Vandals, Avars, and Batavians of the early Middle Ages, which may be classified as 'ethnic groups'.

However, two difficulties complicate this conclusion about the apparently historically recent appearance of the nation. The first difficulty is that these modern developments also contribute to the consolidation and continuation of other traditions of relations that undermine the national community. This first difficulty takes place at two levels: one 'beneath' the nation and the other 'above' the nation. Modern means of communication and public education that clearly are factors in culturally unifying an otherwise diverse population into a modern nation have also contributed to the stabilization and strengthening of regional cultures, especially those with their own languages. This 'regionalism' may lead to the emergence of new nations. Such a possibility can be observed at the beginning of the 21st century in Europe, for example in Slovakia and the Czech Republic, and in the various and many claims to regional autonomy, such as that of Scotland in Great Britain, Euzkadi and Catalan in Spain, and the relation of Corsica to France. These modern, culturally unifying factors have also resulted in developments 'above' the nation that may undermine its existence because they have reinvigorated the tradition of empire, for example the emerging European Union with trans-national institutions such as the European Court of Human Rights.

The second difficulty involves a more nuanced, thus more accurate, appraisal of pre-modern societies. Certainly, the spread of the world religions in antiquity, particularly of Buddhism, Christianity, and, later, Islam, calls into question the extent of the supposed cultural isolation of populations that are presumed to be largely illiterate. I say 'presumed' because there was indeed a significant degree of literacy in a number of ancient societies; ancient Israel as early as the 7th century BCE was a largely literate society. Indeed, archaeologists discovered a piece of pottery from an ancient rural village on which it appears that someone was practising making the letters of the 'proto-Hebrew' alphabet as early as the 12th century BCE.

8. Eighty letters from the 'proto-Hebrew' alphabet (from around 1100 BCE) written on pottery, discovered in 1976 at 'Izbet Sartah

The spread of the world religions in antiquity indicates that extensive relations throughout a vast population and across great distances can indeed be formed in the absence of mass-produced books, newspapers, railways, and markets for industrial goods. Moreover, law codes are to be found throughout antiquity and the Middle Ages, as well as conceptions of territories with fairly precise boundaries. Rather than a sharp historical contrast between ancient and modern relations, there is, for both periods, a much more complicated criss-crossing of attachments, a proper appreciation of which is obscured by such a contrast. The development, however ambiguous, of significant expressions of national community can be found in a number of pre-modern societies. Let us examine additional details of our four examples that indicate such a development.

Formative factors of pre-modern nations

As observed in Chapter 3, law is an important factor in the formation of an extensive, relatively uniform territory. If, as seems likely, the Books of Chronicles of the Hebrew Bible contain a degree of factually reliable evidence, then in ancient Israel the 'Levites' were government officials placed throughout the land to administer the law, both civil and religious, and to collect taxes (2 Chronicles 17:7–9; 19:4–11; 24; see also Deuteronomy 17:9). Furthermore, the Israelite law codes, as we have them in, for example, Leviticus, drew a distinction between the 'native of the land', the Israelite, to whom the law applied, and the foreigner. Significantly, the foreigner who resided permanently in the land is described as being subject to the law of the land as if he had been born there. Finally, it appears that the Israelites established a judicial hierarchy, so that unsettled local disputes could be brought to the centre for final adjudication (Deuteronomy 17:8).

In Japan, during the late 7th and the 8th centuries, there certainly existed pronounced regional distinctions between territorial clans, one indication of which was the civil war of 672 CE. The significance of these distinctions would later increase until finally being undermined, if not by the centralized Tokugawa Shogunate (1603 CE) then by the Meiji Restoration (1868 CE). Despite such regional differences, the emperor remained an unquestioned object of veneration transcending these regional loyalties, even though political authority, beginning in the 12th century, resided not with the emperor but in the office of the 'barbarian-subduing general', the Bakufu of the Shogun. Indicating the existence of a national collective self-consciousness was, during the Tokugawa Period, the combination of the samurai's slogans 'revere the emperor' and 'expel the barbarian'. The basis for such a combination was laid during the 7th and 8th centuries when the influence of the clans was weakened in favour of the centralized authority of the emperor, through the written compilation of extensive codes of laws that were applied throughout the entire country, culminating in what historians refer to as the 'Ritsuryo State'. These laws divided the country into provinces, and established a differentiated ministerial apparatus responsible for household registration, taxes, allocation of rice fields (including to women), military conscription, and religion. Furthermore, social mobility based on achievement rather than birth was possible, often following Chinese practice, the so-called system of 'caps and ranks'; and there were occupational groups that cut across distinction by clan, for example metal workers, scribes, and irrigation specialists.

Religion was an important factor in the development of a distinctive culture in each of these pre-modern societies. The god of Israel was Yahweh, while those countries that bordered Israel had different gods: for Aram to its north, the god Hadad; for Ammon to its northeast, Milcom; for Moab directly to its east, Chemosh; and for Egypt to its south, Horus-Seth (or Amen-Re). Policies of the Israelite centre during the reign of King Josiah (640–609 BCE) sought to make consistent the worship of Yahweh throughout the land, with the Passover Festival and sacrifice allowed only at the Temple in Jerusalem. In Japan, by the late 7th century CE, the emperor's family had appropriated the sun goddess Amaterasu, as not only its divine ancestor but also as being ascendant over all local, clan gods, the *kami*. Furthermore, the Japanese centre, through its 'council of *kami* affairs', controlled the worship of the Shinto *kami* at both the court (including at Ise, the site of the shrine of Amaterasu) and local levels. The centre also constructed throughout Japan Shinto shrines and Buddhist temples, as Buddhism was also under imperial control during this period.

In Sri Lanka, beginning with King Dutthagāmani and continuing throughout the early Anurādhapura period, the ruling centre built Buddhist shrines, especially the impressive *stupas*, throughout the island.

The significance of Roman Catholicism for sustaining the territorial relation of Poland is clear, once one recognizes that Germany to its west was Lutheran and Russia to its east was Orthodox; although there were important religious minorities, Protestant and Jewish, throughout the history of medieval and early modern Poland.

In addition to these legal and religious, territorially unifying developments, in each of these four societies war was another factor in the formation of a distinctive culture. In early Sinhalese history, there was not only the conflict with the Tamils, but also with Hindu forces from southern India. For ancient Israel, there was war with the Philistines and the Ammonites, amongst others. In 663 CE Japan engaged in military conflict with T'ang China (albeit on the Korean peninsula) that resulted, according to Chinese, Korean, and Japanese records, in the defeat of the Japanese. In response to the Chinese victory and out of fear of an impending invasion by Chinese forces, the Japanese undertook a frenzied and massive construction of military defences. For Poland, throughout the 14th century, the restoration of what was viewed as Polish territory under King Łokietek and his son Casimir required successful military campaigns against both the Teutonic Knights and the Czechs. All of these wars required a mass mobilization of the population. Thus, the Japanese legal codes mandated that military units, organized by provinces, consist of one male from each household; under Casimir and afterwards, while military service was by law obligatory for all owners of land, there were instances of significant participation of peasants, as in the final battle with the Teutonic Knights in 1431. These mass mobilizations are reminiscent of Henry II's Assize of Arms (1181), discussed in Chapter 3. What was the influence of these mobilizations for defence and war on the self-understanding of the majority of the population?

Because there is little or no evidence for how the peasantry experienced and understood these wars, some scholars assume that the peasants did not view such conflicts as wars between nations. Given the above discussion, how likely is this assumption? It is difficult to avoid suspecting that, given developments such as a territorially unifying religion and law propagated by the ruling centre, found in varying degrees in all of these societies, there must have been some degree of recognition by the peasantry that the centre of their respective society was precisely that, and accordingly was due their respect, even if the centre was experienced, as it often is for modern nations, as being burdensome (for example in terms of taxes). In each of these four examples, there existed an authoritative centre: Anurādhapura for Sri Lanka, Jerusalem for Israel, Nara for Japan, and Cracow for Poland. In contrast to these examples, one reason why ancient Greece never developed into a nation is that, despite numerous indications of a pan-Hellenic self-consciousness during the wars with Persia, an authoritative centre capable of propagating and sustaining that self-consciousness through the existence of pan-Hellenic institutions, at the expense of loyalty primarily to the city-states, did not emerge. It does seem likely that during times of war the vast majority of the populations in the pre-modern societies of our four examples viewed the conflict as being between 'native' and foreigner. Certainly, the subsequent history of the ancient Israelites, the wars against Rome from 66 to 72 CE and from 132 to 135 CE that involved the entire population, justifies this possibility.

In addition to religion and law, language was also a factor contributing to the formation of these pre-modern national communities. In Israelite tradition there is evidence that suggests that differences in language may have been understood as indicating distinctions between native Israelites and foreigners (2 Kings 18:26; see also Judges 12:6 and Genesis 10:4,20). We can be more confident about differences in language being understood as representing national differences in the history of medieval Poland, when there had developed acute anti-German sentiment. After the presumed German-led revolt of Cracow against Łokietek was put down in 1312, the guilt of its instigators was determined by whether or not they could correctly pronounce such Polish words as *soczewica* (lentil), *koło* (wheel), and *młyn* (mill). The person who was unable to do so was judged to be either German or Czech and, hence, guilty.

Complications

Nevertheless, in our examples, the relation between native and foreigner could at times become blurred. We know, for example, that during the 7th century CE, in the aftermath of the Chinese military victories against the Korean kingdoms, many Koreans fled to Japan. However, significantly, it would appear that by the next century these immigrants, many of whom were Buddhists, had been incorporated into the mythological kinship of the Japanese through the imperial registry of families. Somewhat similar complications can be observed in the traditions of ancient Israel. Despite the portrayal of a restricted Israelite kinship found in the Books of Ezra and Nehemiah that went so far as to prohibit intermarriage, after the Judaean leader Hyrcanus I (125 BCE) conquered Idumea (Edom), the Idumeans became a part of the Jewish nation.

> Hyrcanus subdued all the Idumeans; and permitted them to stay in that country, if they would circumcise their genitals, and make use of the laws of the Jews. They were so desirous of living in the country of their forefathers, that they submitted to circumcision, and the rest of the Jewish ways of living; at which time therefore this befell them, that they were hereafter no other than Jews.
>
> Josephus, *The Antiquities of the Jews*

In both of these cases, one observes how war may be a factor in the formation of a territorial kinship. To be sure, where territories are not geographically isolated, as they are in the 'island nations' of Japan and Sri Lanka, determination of the national territory and, thus, the kinship of the nation is especially complicated, specifically in the border regions, for example, in the case of Poland, in the area of Silesia with its German-speaking population.

Despite such complications, all of these pre-modern societies had to one degree or another the following characteristics that justify considering them to be nations:

(1) a self-designating name;

(2) a written history;

(3) a degree of cultural uniformity, often as a result of and sustained by religion;

(4) legal codes;

(5) an authoritative centre, and

(6) a conception of a bounded territory.

However, examinations of all of these societies also indicate uneven developments of each of these characteristics constitutive of a nation. Even the most elementary feature of the existence of the collective self-consciousness of a nation, its self-designating name, can be ambiguous, as was the case for perhaps the clearest example of a pre-modern nation, ancient Israel. At times the designation 'Israel' referred to: the kingdom of David and Solomon; the northern kingdom of Israel, as distinct from the southern kingdom of Judah; and often as a goal to be realized.

Moreover, during much of the period of the Second Temple (538 BCE to 70 CE), the ideal of Israel was borne by the society designated as Judea. The ambiguity of the self-designating name of the nation, often indicating sharply competing visions of what the nation is and should be, can be found today in, for example, 'Mother India', which may or may not be understood to include Christians, Muslims, and Sikhs. However, this does not mean that, today, legally, religiously, and linguistically diverse India is not a nation. Granted these and other complications, those characteristics that suggest the existence of a bounded, territorial community of kinship in earlier periods should not be denied.

The criterion of citizenship

It is sometimes argued that the criterion for the existence of a national community should be citizenship. Let us consider this possibility by returning to the medieval history of Poland. If one insists that a citizenship that extends to the vast majority of the population should be the decisive criterion for the existence of a nation, then medieval Poland was not a nation. It was at most a 'nation of the nobility', for it was the nobility that determined, beginning in the 15th century through its parliament, the *Sejm*, the political affairs of medieval Poland. However, this criterion of citizenship raises a number of complications for the historian for his or her understanding of such modern nations as England and France of the 19th century.

If there is hesitation in characterizing medieval Poland as a nation because full civil and political participation was limited to the nobility, then should not the same reservations apply to England and France – by 1832, only 3.2% of the population in England was entitled to vote for parliament and only 1.5% in France was enfranchised? Moreover, if one insists that a nation exists only where there are recognized legal rights and duties common to the vast majority of the population, then one is in a quandary as to how to characterize stateless Poland during the 19th century, when its territory was partitioned between Prussia, Austria, and Russia. During this period there certainly continued to exist a Polish collective self-consciousness.

There can be no doubt that democracy, as a form of government for making decisions, facilitates the stability of the nation as a territorial community precisely because it recognizes legal rights and political participation for the vast majority of the population. Nevertheless, to elevate modern conceptions of citizenship as the criterion for the existence of a nation collapses the nation as a territorial relation of kinship into one form for making political decisions. The historian who insists on the criterion of citizenship for the existence of a nation and who thereby maintains the distinction between pre-modern societies and modern nations is thus forced to:

(1) minimize significant and continuing expressions of territorial relations of kinship in pre-modern societies;

(2) overestimate the cultural uniformity of the modern nation; and

(3) invite an analytical quandary in light of such developments as stateless nations and 'regionalism'.

To be sure, the conclusion that there existed pre-modern nations requires that the analyst tolerate various ambiguities, various partial developments; but in reality the nation as a social relation is always a fluid combination of a criss-crossing plurality of different and developing relations. This is also the case for the modern national state, where even the determination of membership is subject to an ongoing process of reinterpretation, as can be seen in the changing laws of immigration and citizenship (for example, the 1971 and 1981 UK Nationality Acts, and the 1990 US Immigration Act).

There are, nonetheless, differences to be observed between the structures of pre-modern and modern territorial relations of kinship. The sociologists Edward Shils and S. N. Eisenstadt rightly emphasized that modern societies are characterized by a greater participation of the peripheral sections of society in the activities of the centre, thereby indicating a greater cultural cohesiveness of the territorial relation. Examples of such participation are democracy where sovereignty ultimately resides in the majority of the population, public education, and an increased social mobility as a result of personal achievement rather than a rigidly maintained social hierarchy based on the status derived from the circumstances of birth. However, the historical differences in the relation of periphery to centre between modern nations and our four examples are better understood as a question of degree because of the existence in the latter of written codes of law, conceptions that the king was responsible for the society (to maintain irrigation systems, to maintain the law, to maintain the peace), and the centre's many obligations to the national religion, such as the construction of shrines, temples, and churches.

Clearly, the difference between a popularly elected prime minister or president and a king is important. However, a king has also been an object of respect, and, as such, a point of reference in the collective self-consciousness of a territorial relation of kinship, for example the Japanese emperor or the French king as a miraculous healer of the sick, as described by the historian Marc Bloch. To be sure, it is likely that the firmness, the prominence, of the territorial relation, as expressed by the sentiment of patriotism, is greater when the distinction between periphery and centre is not acute; but this does not mean that the consciousness of defending the home was not extended beyond the familial home to the homeland of the pre-modern society. Such an extension, and the territorial community that it implies, was made possible by the recognition of the centre, for example of the king, as the defender of the peace of the country, shared customs (including religion and language), and histories that contained mythical elements.

We conclude this chapter by returning to the consideration of mythical elements in the formation of the nation. It may be possible for a bounded society to be formed on a purely contractual basis; but it has not happened yet. This is not to deny the importance of the European, constitutional tradition of an agreement between the governed and the ruler, and especially that both are subject to the law. Nonetheless, in the formation of modern territorial relations, a distant, often mythical past, or an asserted empirically unverifiable condition, has been appealed to time and again to justify the uniqueness of those relations.

Such an appeal may amount to little more than a cynical calculation for the purpose of exploiting communal tensions. In India, for example, there was the 8-year-long campaign by the Hindu Rashtriya Swayamsevak Sangh and the Bharatiya Janata Party to demolish the 475-year-old Muslim mosque at Ayodhya, culminating in its destruction on 6 December 1992, because it was supposedly the place of the birth of Ram, the incarnation of the Hindu god Vishnu, of the epic *Ramayana*, much of which was probably written more than 2,000 years ago. The appeal to the past may be more of a creation than a restoration, for example the revival of the Shinto religion in Japan beginning in the 18th century that culminated in the 'State Shinto' of the Meiji Restoration (1868). In both of these instances, myths were exploited in the service of infusing a nationalistic vision into the territorial relation – for India, the idea of *Hindutva* ('Hinduness'); for Japan, that of *Kokutai* (a 'national essence'). Both sought to deny historically factual complications in the formation of the nation that a more civil conception of a territorial relation would tolerate: for India, Sikhs in Punjab, Christians in Kerala, and Muslims in Kashmir who contradict a vision of India as necessarily Hindu; for Japan, a more than 1,400-year-long history of Buddhism that contradicts a vision of Japan as free from foreign influence.

The appeal to the past may be rather obscure. For example, a monument known as the *Hermannsdenkmal* was constructed in 1875 in the Teutoburger Forest, near Detmold in North Rhine-Westphalia, Germany, to commemorate the victory in 9 CE of Arminius, or Hermann, warlord of the Cherusci, over the Roman armies under the command of Quinctilius Varus. The monument was to represent the independence of the German nation, asserting a factually most doubtful kinship between the ancient Cherusci and modern Germans.

The appeal to the same past may differ depending upon the circumstances of the present. In 1989, as tensions were escalating with the Croats that would soon erupt into a genocidal war, the Serbs celebrated the 600th anniversary of the Battle of Kosovo, when in 1389 under the command of Prince Lazar they were defeated by the Ottoman Empire; and yet in 1939, facing the prospect of German invasion, there were attempts to portray the battle as a symbol of the independence not of Serbia but of Yugoslavia.

Elements of myth are also to be observed in the traditions of the United States of America, and not merely in the propositions of the

9. The *Hermannsdenkmal*

Declaration of Independence about the 'self-evident truths' that 'all men are created equal' having been 'endowed by their Creator with certain unalienable rights' that are ultimately derived from a Judaeo-Christian heritage. As the American tradition has developed, there has arisen a myth of the founding fathers of the nation that obscures any number of differences between them about the implications of these statements of equality and rights, for example whether self-rule was to be federal or national. Some of the controversies arising from these ambiguities were uneasily settled by the American Civil War, in favour of – as is often the result of war – an increased national unity. However, new myths emerged, such as the belief in the 'manifest destiny' of the American people to establish the boundaries of the nation from the Atlantic to the Pacific. Indeed, it was argued that these boundaries were designated by God, even though, as with the ancient Israelites, there was uncertainty as to their location, specifically whether the northwest boundary should be the 49th parallel or further north at 54,40.

These latter cases of modern India, Japan, Germany, Serbia, and the United States represent only a few of many possible examples that indicate that in the formation and continuation of all nations, including those of the modern world, there are appeals to ideas, such as a trans-generational territorial kinship or 'truth' or 'unalienable rights'. Such ideas, while not capable of empirical verification, provide justification for the bounded social order. The most obvious example of a set of ideas that cannot be empirically verified is religion. In all of the territorial relations of kinship, both pre-modern and modern, discussed in this chapter, religion has been a factor in their formation and continued existence. The problem to be taken up now is therefore an examination of the relation between the nation and religion.

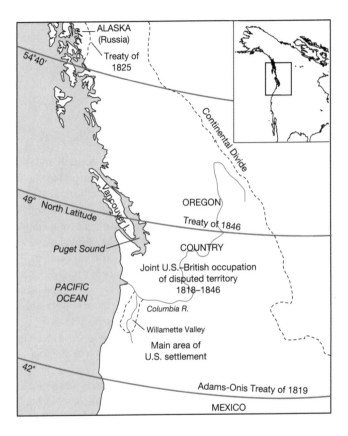

10. The Oregon territory before 1846, indicating the uncertainty of the
northwest border of the United States

Chapter 6
Whose god is mightier?

The relation between the nation and religion is historically and conceptually complicated. Religion has both been integral to, and at odds with, the formation and continuation of nations. An understanding of this relation requires a determination of how it varies from one religion to another, thereby entailing a comparative analysis. Let us begin the examination of this complicated relationship by returning to the previous chapter's four cases, in each of which religion is integral to the existence of a nation.

Although the origin of the nation of ancient Israel is, as with other nations, obscure, it is likely that an important element in its formation was the war camp. What little evidence we have about its early history, for example the monument of Pharaoh Merneptah (1207 BCE) that records the victory of Egypt over a people designated as 'Israel', or such 'proto-Israelite' military alliances as described in Judges 5, suggests as much. The likelihood of such a possibility is increased if the disputed etymology of the term 'Israel' is, in fact, 'god (El) contends'.

While one cannot say with certainty when the worship of Yahweh became dominant among the deities worshipped by that population that was becoming 'Israel', it is probable that Yahweh was the god of David and Solomon. Certainly at some point in Israelite history, to be an Israelite (or Judaean) was to worship

11. The monument of Pharaoh Merneptah, containing the statement that 'Israel is laid waste and his seed is not' because of the military victory of Egypt in *circa* 1207 BCE

Yahweh, thereby distinguishing the Israelites from the Milcom-worshipping Ammonites, the Chemosh-worshipping Moabites, and the Hadad-worshipping Aramaeans. Moreover, clearly the worship of Yahweh sustained the existence of the Jewish nation throughout the Babylonian, Persian, Seleucid, and Roman occupations.

The worship of primarily one god by one society, for example Yahweh by the Israelites or Chemosh by the Moabites, thereby excluding the worship of the god of another society without denying its existence, represents a significant development for the existence of a nation. In this instance, where worship of a god is limited to a territory and the people of that territory, religion and nation coincide with one another, such a religion sustains the nation, because the worship of such a god, as the 'god of the land', unifies the land and its inhabitants into the culturally relatively uniform territorial community of the nation. It is only with monotheism that, at least doctrinally, the existence of other gods is denied as they are judged to be false idols. However, even when the ancient Israelites became monotheists, the worship of Yahweh by the ancient Israelites and later by the Jews continued to contain the ideas of a chosen people, promised land, and supposed lineage of Abraham-Isaac-and Jacob that distinguished these monotheists, as a nation, from the other children of the one and only god.

As we have observed, early on and continuing throughout Sinhalese history, the uneven territorial unification of Sri Lanka was inseparable from the propagation of Buddhism throughout the island. The continued history of Japan as Japan, above all the institution of the emperor, rests to no small degree on the worship of the Japanese deities, the territorial *kami* of the clans, and the transformation of that worship into a national religion through the worship of the sun goddess Amaterasu. Finally, while the 14th-century CE Polish kingdoms of Łokietek and his son Casimir had as their reference the restoration of the territory of the Piast kingdom,

Roman Catholicism was central to that restoration, initially as a Papal protectorate and subsequently by distinguishing Poland from Lutheran Germany on its western border and Eastern Orthodox Russia on its eastern border.

In all of these cases, as well as others such as the conversion of ancient Armenia to Christianity and the formation of the societies of Eastern Orthodoxy, the role of religion as a factor in the emergence and continuation of the relative territorial cohesion of these previously culturally fragmented societies into nations was abetted by the political policies of the emerging and then authoritative centres. Nevertheless, there were complications in religion's contribution to the cohesiveness of these nations. For example, for ancient Israel there were Yahweh-worshipping Samaritans during the period of the Second Temple; for Japan, Buddhism was important throughout much of its history; for Buddhist Sri Lanka, there were Hindu-worshipping Tamils and numerous aspects of Hinduism incorporated into Sinhalese Buddhism; for Catholic Poland, there were notable Jewish and Protestant minorities.

The nation and monotheism

It tends to be through religion that the individual formulates the purpose of his or her existence; often the relation of his or her society to other societies; and, thus, the place of the individual and his or her society in the perceived order of the universe. However, in the formulation of this purpose, the relation between the nation and religion becomes complicated when that religion is monotheistic. This is because the belief in one, universal god asserts the unity of humanity, and not the distinctiveness of the nation.

The universal monotheism of the ancient Israelites and Jews is explicitly qualified by the two concepts of a 'chosen people' and a 'promised land'. These two concepts join together two purposes to human existence:

1) the continuation of a nation based on the preoccupation with vitality (Deuteronomy 30:19–20, 'choose life, so that you and your children may live . . . in the land'); and

2) the affirmation of a proper order of life that is universal, as conveyed by the belief in one god.

Such a qualification of monotheism need not be conceptually explicit. For example, monotheistic Roman Catholicism and Buddhism, when viewed from the perspective of the respective histories of Poland and Sri Lanka, are also instances where monotheistic beliefs have been intertwined with the nation. Indeed, today, the Sinhalese Buddhists worship the territorial 'Four Warrant Gods' as protectors of the nation.

Consideration of additional evidence will clarify the complicated relation between monotheism and the nation. Eastern Orthodox tradition has it that the Virgin Mary, during the siege of Constantinople by the Avars and Persians in the 6th and early 7th centuries CE, fought alongside the defenders of the city before the walls of the church at Blachernae in which her shroud had supposedly earlier been placed. As a consequence, the view emerged that Mary, Theotokos, 'she who gave birth to God', was the protectress of Constantinople. Polish tradition has it that, in 1655, the Virgin Mary appeared on the walls of the monastery of Częstochowa to defeat the Swedish invaders of Poland. Thus, the belief developed that Mary was the protectress of the territorial integrity of Poland.

There are many examples of a god or goddess being viewed as the guardian of a territorial society. Perhaps the best known is the goddess Athena as benefactress and protectress of ancient Athens; but, of course, ancient Greek religion was polytheistic. However, the beliefs in the supposed actions of the other-worldly Mary at Częstochowa, or those of the Buddha in Sinhalese myth, are examples of monotheistic religions contributing to the consolidation and continuation of spatial limits of significance – the

12. The Virgin Mary of Częstochowa (the 'Black Madonna'). In 1717, Mary was proclaimed by the Polish King Casimir to be Queen of Poland

bounded territory of the this-worldly nation. Should such contributions be understood as a polytheistic compromise of monotheism? After all, why should the 'Mother of God' show preference for Poland, as Athena did for Athens?

Let us consider the complications posed by the nation to monotheism from a different angle. Many nations acknowledge past, critical moments and heroic sacrifices in defence of the nation by having a 'tomb of the unknown soldier'; for example England does so at Westminster Abbey in London, France at the Arc de Triomphe in Paris, the United States at Arlington National Cemetery near Washington, DC, and Japan at the Yasukuni shrine in Tokyo. These tombs are monuments to the nameless territorial ancestors and heroes of the nation who, because they gave their lives protecting their nation in war, are believed to be deserving of veneration.

13. The Yasukuni shrine in Tokyo, built in 1869 to honour the divine spirits of those who sacrificed their lives for Japan in war

Within the monotheistic civilizations, the fallen soldiers commemorated by the 'tomb of the unknown soldier' are not prayed to as gods. These soldiers were of this world; while the Virgin Mary, to whom one may pray, is an other-worldly power. This distinction is important because with the other-worldly Mary, we are in the conceptual world of religion. Nonetheless, a kind of religious aura surrounds the 'tomb of the unknown soldier', thus blurring this distinction.

The imaginative object of the monotheistic religions transcends this world; it is either an other-worldly existence – heaven, Nirvana, or an end of time when the world will be transformed – or an other-worldly power. There are certainly also imaginative elements in the nation, as expressed both in the asserted temporal continuity between the present and the past and in the territorially extensive kinship, both of which are beyond the physical experience of any particular individual. However, the object of this transcendence, the territorial community of the nation, is of this world. Nonetheless, we have already observed examples in which the historical communities of the monotheistic religions have blurred this distinction between the other world and this world. They have repeatedly accommodated themselves to the territorial relations of this world. It is to one such accommodation, also involving the tombs of heroes, that we now turn.

The cult of the saints

In opposition to such accommodations, early Christianity rightly ridiculed the worship of the Roman Caesars as gods. It objected to this pagan elevation of the living human to the divine, an earlier version of which was the worship of the dead Greek hero. Yet, throughout the history of late-antique and medieval Christianity, a variation of this elevation can be observed in the 'cult of the saints'. The cult of the saints often represented an accommodation of monotheism to the nation. How so?

The altar is a specific location where the worshipper seeks access to god; where there is a vertical relation between the worshipper and the heavenly divine. With the cult of the saints, the tomb of the saint becomes another location where the worshipper seeks access to the divine; thus, tomb and altar are in a sense joined. However, when the saint is also a heroic representative of the nation, the divine ceases to be exclusively heavenly. The relation between worshipper and national saint is no longer merely vertical; it becomes also horizontal because the sacredness of the heavenly saint is now understood to contain reference to the nation. The sacredness of the national saint is viewed as pervading the territory of the nation, the very existence of which his or her actions made possible.

Consider, for example, King Louis of France (1226–70 CE), who was canonized in 1297 CE. Clearly, with the canonization of Louis IX, the ruling family of France, the Capetians, became joined to heaven, thereby adding religious legitimacy to their dynastic rule. Various parts of the saintly King Louis were placed, as relics, in different monasteries throughout the territory of France, thereby adding religious support to the territorial unity of the kingdom. One is reminded of both the account of the scattering of the body of Saint Stanisław throughout the territory of Poland and the relics of the Buddha placed in different shrines throughout Sri Lanka.

The jurisdiction of the perceived power of the dead Greek hero who had ascended to Olympus was in the land of the city-state where his bones were buried. This 'territorialization' of supernatural power is similar to that of the Christian national saint, except the land is that of the nation, the entire extent of which now has a relation to the divine, especially so when power-bearing parts of the body are scattered, as religious relics, throughout the land. When the king or hero of a nation becomes a saint, the nation is joined to the eternal order of the universe, thereby contributing to the justification of its territorially bounded, cultural distinctiveness.

The nation and paganism

Monotheism's accommodation to the nation – as presented here by the examples of Mary as the protectress of Poland paralleling the pagan goddess Athena's relation to ancient Athens, and the variation of the pagan elevation of the human to the divine in the cult of the saints – leads to posing a provocative question. Does the nation today represent the continuation of paganism within the civilizations of our time to which monotheism has accommodated itself? The answer to this question will depend upon how the term 'pagan' is understood. The word is from the Latin *paganus* that, for the Romans, meant belonging to the countryside or to a village, hence a peasant. As the early Christians tended to live in cities, the term 'pagan' came to mean someone who, because he or she lived in the countryside, was presumed not to be Christian; and perhaps the rural population remained more faithful to the polytheistic nature deities. (Here one observes the tradition of associating the peasantry with the gods of nature and fertility, of the land – a tradition that received its fullest expression with those 19th-century Romantics who thought that the 'true nation' resided with the peasantry.)

Characteristic of paganism was that, in the words of the pagan Symmachus, Prefect of Rome (384 CE), 'each people is given its own divine power to take care of its destiny', just as the Athenians had the goddess Athena. After the Emperor Augustus, this supernatural power (which the Romans called their *genius*) had been attributed to the Roman emperor, because he was the one responsible for the destiny of the Roman people. This development reached its logical conclusion in the elevation of the emperor to a god. Thus, as the emperor, as head of the state, was divine, so, too, the state itself became divine. In the aftermath of Fascism and Communism, the term 'paganism' has sometimes been used to refer to the deification of the state, where nothing is held to be more important than the state. This is a reasonable usage, signifying the horrors unleashed upon humanity when, because the state is elevated above all other concerns and, thus, is worshipped as if it were a god, the humane truths of monotheism – particularly that all of humanity is created in the image of god – are repudiated.

However, I wish to put all this aside and focus on what, for our purposes, is also conveyed by the term 'paganism': the recognition of the gods of both the ancestors and the land. These pagan gods are the symbolic expression of the territorial relation of nativity. They are the gods of nature, of vitality and its transmission, whose jurisdiction, like that of the national saint, is territorially limited; and who, as such, are to be contrasted with the universality of the god of monotheism. To be sure, such gods are not openly acknowledged today within our monotheistic civilizations. Nevertheless, are not the pagan ideas of the gods of the land and ancestors implicitly conveyed in today's conceptions of a fatherland and motherland? In so far as the nation is a bounded territorial community of nativity, is it not a bearer of these pagan ideas within monotheistic civilization? After all, much of European history, including the 20th century, was a history of one Christian nation engaged in war with another Christian nation, each defending its own perceived, unique relation to the divine. And, indeed, many Christian lands have their respective national saints. The recognition of national saints represents the homage paid by the otherwise universalistic, monotheistic religions to the territorial kinship of the nation.

I have observed that, in the formation and continuation of any social relation, numerous and different pursuits and interests are intertwined with one another. Certainly, one factor in the accommodation of the monotheistic religions to the territorial relation (that may be characterized by the religious category 'pagan') has been a concern for adding support, hence stability, to political power through religion. This was obviously so in the French King Philip the Fair's exploitation of the cult of his grandfather, Louis IX, in the emergence of France as a nation; in the ancient Israelite King Josiah's centralization of the cult of Yahweh that served to establish Jerusalem as the political centre of the Israelite nation; in King Dutthagāmani propagation of Buddhism at the expense of the Hindu Tamils; in the 'territorialization' of Christianity through the principle of *cuius regio, eius religio* (only one form of Christianity in a territory, depending upon the faith of the ruler) of the Augsburg Treaty of 1555 CE; and in the Moroccan cult of the Islamic Idris, championed by the Marinids in the 14th and 15th centuries CE to further the image of Morocco at the expense of tribal loyalties. In all of these examples, monotheism has been adapted to serve the consolidation of nations.

Rather than insisting on a sharp historical contrast between pagan religions and monotheistic religions, it is more accurate to recognize two evidently persistent religious patterns of orientation that come together in varying ways. Clearly, the relation between monotheism and the nation can be tension-filled, and aggravatingly so when it achieves the institutional expression of a separation between church and state. In the face of an enormous amount of historically complicated evidence, the problem becomes one of clarifying the variation of the relation between the nation and religion from one civilization to another.

Comparison by civilizations

The tension between the nation and religion is lessened when the religion itself is territorially restricted; that is, when there is a 'god of the land', as in many of the ancient, polytheistic religions. There are several observations about this relation in antiquity to be made.

It was common then for the gods to be appeased by worshippers through sacrifice, in the expectation that they would bestow favour in return. For example, sacrifice was made to the gods of fertility, such as the storm god Baal of ancient Ugarit, Hadad of the Aramaeans, and the Hittite Telipinu, in the hope that they would bring rain so that there would be a bountiful crop. Droughts were understood to be a result of the gods' withdrawal of favour or even their absence.

When the storm god is also the war god, a religious development has occurred. The combining of functions (in this case, rain and war) indicates that a greater coherence in religious understanding has taken place, because the conceptual chaos arising from the existence of many gods, each with their own function, has been lessened. One observes an anticipation of this development in the Babylonian creation myth, the *Enuma Elish*, where it is asserted that although there are fifty gods, each with their own name and function, they are all one god, Marduk. This coherence, when accompanied by a stable pantheon, represents a development of a relative cultural uniformity – a development often marked in religious myth by a war between the younger gods against the older, as in the Mesopotamian and Greek traditions. Such a relative cultural uniformity does not necessarily signify the existence of a nation; both ancient Sumeria and ancient Greece lacked an authoritative centre capable of subordinating loyalties to the particular city-states to, respectively, Sumeria and Greece as nations. Nonetheless, such a relative, bounded cultural uniformity is noteworthy as a development towards the nation.

When this relatively greater coherence of religious conception is accompanied by the ascendancy of the god of the land within the pantheon, then that cultural uniformity is explicitly territorial. For example, the Egyptian worship of Horus (Lower Egypt)-Seth (Upper Egypt), and later Amen (Theban)-Re, may indicate the existence of a nation. When the god of the land is the primary god to be worshipped, then such a religion likely signifies the existence of a nation, as there exists a collective self-consciousness that a people has its land, that land has its people, and both that people and that land are unified respectively into a nation and a territory through the worship of the god of that people and that land.

> There were foreign rites established among the Caunians, but later they turned against them and resolved to follow none but their own gods; and so all the Caunians, putting on their armor – all, that is, of military age – advanced to the boundaries of their country, beating the air with their spears and saying that they were driving out the gods of the foreigners.
>
> Herodotus, *The History*

These developments in the religions of antiquity could, however, follow different paths that would complicate the relation between the nation and religion. When the image of the god that had heretofore been a factor in the assertion of the cultural distinctiveness of a territorially bounded society acquired the attributes of other gods (a process known as 'syncretism'), above all, those of other societies, then that distinctiveness was undermined. An example of such a syncretism was the cult of the Egyptian Isis that spread throughout the Mediterranean world. Moreover, under the impact of the philosophies of Stoicism and neo-Platonism, there arose religions that could be characterized as 'pagan monotheism', the classic example of which was the Roman Emperor Julian's worship of the sun. Rather than serving the consolidation and continued existence of a nation, religious syncretism and pagan monotheism contributed to the existence of an empire.

Regarding the monotheistic religions, as Judaism's relation to the nation has already been discussed, only a few additional comments are required before turning to Christianity and Islam.

Monotheistic Judaism's intimate relation to the nation is a consequence of the universal orientation of the belief, requiring a 'circumcision of the heart' (Deuteronomy 30:6), in one god who created all of humanity in his image (Genesis 1:27) being explicitly combined with the assertion of the cultural distinctiveness of the beliefs in a chosen people and a promised land. Judaism's conceptual development of one, universal god who intervened into the history of humanity by forming a relationship with a particular nation has had a profound influence on Western civilization. This influence consists of:

1) beliefs of other nations, for example the French during the Middle Ages, that they were 'chosen';
2) a conception of time as directional, exhibiting progress, but one that nonetheless continued to contain returns to past moments that were perceived to have established various forms of national distinctiveness, ranging from the covenant between Yahweh and the Israelites at Mount Sinai, to the Puritan emigration to the new promised land of America, to Poland as the sacrificial saviour of Christendom; and
3) a conception of the end of time when the rupture between

this world and the other world would be overcome, thereby re-establishing Eden.

This religious development combined, albeit uneasily, universal monotheism with the nation in such a way that a particular nation was viewed by its members as being different ('chosen') precisely because its existence was understood as being uniquely related to the universal purpose of the god of all of humanity. As a consequence, in Judaism one finds the belief that not only is Israel sustained by its centre, Jerusalem, but that Jerusalem is also the centre of the world (Ezekiel 5:5, Jubilees 8:19) because it is there where the world is joined to God. Such a belief is to be found, with variation, in other civilizations. For example, in Eastern Orthodoxy, there arose the belief that Moscow was the 'Third Rome', and, as such, should be the centre not only of Russia but also of universal Christianity. There thus arises an understanding that the nation has an historic mission in the transformation of the world.

However, the assertion of universal significance of the centre, such as Jerusalem or Moscow, carries with it the potential to break the limitation of the cultural distinctiveness of the nation in favour of empire. An example of this potential is to be found in Confucian China of the Han Empire (202 BCE to 220 CE). The Chinese centre, *zhongguo*, was understood to be responsible for the dispersion of the proper civilized way of life, *li*, that could, in principle, be accepted by anyone. Indeed, it was believed that the emperor ruled with the mandate of heaven only if he combined *li*, through the correct performance of ritual, with a correctly disciplined heart. The most obvious religious expressions of this universalistic orientation at the expense of national attachments are Roman Catholicism and Islam, with their respective centres of Rome and Mecca.

In contrast to the ancient Israelite and Jewish beliefs in the supposed lineage of Abraham-Isaac-and-Jacob and the territory of the promised land, Paul rejected such attachments.

> Here there is no Greek or Jew, circumcised or uncircumcised, barbarian, Scythian, slave or free, but Christ is all, and is in all.
>
> **Colossians 3:11**

Christianity is doctrinally a universal religion whose homeland is not of this world. One would thus expect Christianity to be at odds with the nation. Indeed, Christianity recognizes a distinction between this world, that of Caesar, and the other world, that of God. To be sure, Jesus's distinction between these two realms (Matthew 22:21) was ambiguous, and rendered more so as it underwent interpretation under the demands of future events.

However, because Christianity has recognized this distinction between the 'city of man' and the 'city of God', there exists an arena, the city of man, for the development of the relations of kinship of the nation. Nonetheless, the otherwise oppositional universalism of Paul remains, thereby posing the problem of the relation between these two realms. Viewed from the perspective of the nation, the doctrinal victory, during the 2nd century CE, of the early Church over the Gnostic Marcion (who opposed including the Hebrew scriptures, with their ideas of a chosen people and promised land, as part of the Christian Bible) was to legitimate, albeit uneasily and paradoxically, this arena for national attachments to develop. Thus, the relation between Christianity and the nation in the history of Christian civilization has gravitated between two poles:

1) where Christianity and the nation have come together in different ways; for example, the national churches of both Eastern Orthodoxy and Protestantism, the recognition of national saints, and the belief that various Christian nations are 'chosen'; and

2) an imperial tradition, for example the Christian Roman empire, the

Holy Roman Empire of early and medieval Europe, and Moscow as the Third Rome.

Similar to Judaism and Christianity, Islam recognizes a distinction between this world and the other world. However, unlike Christianity, the Muslim community is obligated to transform this world in accordance with its universal image of the other world. In this regard, the Muslim community, through obedience to its sacred law, the *Shari'ah*, followed ancient Judaism, as the Jews are to be a 'kingdom of priests and a holy nation' (Exodus 19:6) in this world. The crucial difference between Judaism and Islam with regard to the nation is that the Jews are to be a holy nation, while the Islamic community, the *ummah*, is envisioned as being universal. For Judaism, the attachments to kinship and territory are explicit, although they co-exist uneasily with a belief in a god whose jurisdiction was the entire world. For Christianity, a conceptual arena for their existence, the city of man, was recognized, but not without difficulty. For Islam, however, there is an overt opposition to recognizing as legitimate these attachments.

The intention of this comparison is to recognize only a tendency in the variability for the emergence and continued existence of nations in different civilizations, classified by their respective religions. Clearly, many factors other than religious have had a bearing on the existence of nations, such as relative geographical isolation, as in Japan and Sri Lanka. However, the task of this chapter is to isolate religion as a factor in the emergence and continued existence of nations; and it is evident that when compared to Christian civilization, the history of Islamic civilization, until the late 19th and 20th centuries, is not one of a number of national societies.

Yet the contrast is not absolute, and not only because Christian civilization also has a tradition of empire. One is, for example, struck by the historian of the civilization of the early and medieval Islamic Middle East Ibn Khaldûn's repeated use in *The Muqaddimah*, written in 1377 CE, of the concept of 'group feeling' or 'solidarity' (*'asabiyya*), signifying the collective self-consciousness of kinship beyond its literal reference to the family to include the attachments found to one's neighbours, allies, and state (dynasty). Justifying Ibn Khaldûn's use of this concept to indicate the social relation of a territorially extensive kinship within the Islamic Middle East is the long history of Iran. For example, one observes:

1) the resilience of the term *īrāniyyat*, 'being a Persian', in contrast to being an Arab;
2) the Persian Buyids' (945–1060 CE) opposition to the Arab rule of the Abbasids, underscored by the former's introduction of the ancient Iranian title of the *Shah*; and
3) beginning in the early 16th century, Iran's adoption, under the Safawids, of Shi'ism in opposition to the Ottoman Empire's Sunni beliefs.

In the western part of the Islamic Middle East, political and cultural conflicts arose between the Maghrib of North Africa and Muslim Spain; and in the 17th century CE, military clashes occurred between Muslim Morocco and the Muslim Ottomans.

Finally, Islam, too, has had its veneration of saints, although not without opposition. To be sure, this 'pagan element' within Islam did not always have territorial implications; but it occasionally facilitated territorial solidarities within Islamic civilization when the saints were of a local dynasty. This was the case in the Moroccan cult of the *sharifs*, the supposed descendants of Muhammad through the 8th-century CE Idris. In the formation of Morocco, both the Marinids and especially the 'Alawites (17th to 18th centuries CE) claimed authority as *sharifs* that served as an ideal of a unified Islamic Morocco in contrast to local tribal loyalties. Nonetheless, the this-worldly universalism of Islam has tended to be an obstacle to the consolidation and extension of local attachments into nations throughout much of the history of the Islamic Middle East.

Chapter 7
Human divisiveness

Throughout history, humans have understood and organized themselves in different ways. There have been world, monotheistic religions, in which humanity is understood to be one. There have been universal empires such as the Roman, in which citizenship was common to many of their inhabitants. And there have been nations. The ethically pressing philosophical and anthropological puzzle is that humans often organize themselves divisively into various forms of kinship, of which the nation is one example. Why do humans classify themselves in categories of relatedness that are limited, rather than universal? This problem of human divisiveness, posed by the very existence of nations, is the subject of this chapter.

Some analysts of the divisions of humanity have thought that there is something 'given' or 'natural' about those divisions. Moreover, many members of nations believe that there is something given about the existence of their own nation and, although it is of less concern to them, about the existence of other nations of which they are not members. The phrase 'something given' is obviously ambiguous. Those who wish to understand the divisiveness of humanity must certainly clarify the ambiguity of this belief. However, they must also seek to understand why this belief has been so significant to those who hold it.

Race?

During the 19th and first half of the 20th centuries, there were those who thought that the divisions of humanity were 'given' in the sense that they were an unavoidable consequence of racial differences. For example, the French diplomat Arthur de Gobineau (1816–82) argued that humanity was divided into different races and, furthermore, that these races determined the distinctiveness of the culture of one civilization from that of another. His arguments had been anticipated by the vaguely racialist views of the brothers Johannes and Olaus Magnus (mid-16th century) on the Goths, and Richard Verstegan on the English (1605); but it was Gobineau who developed more clearly the view that the decline of a civilization was the inevitable result of the mixing of one race with another. This view was subsequently extended by the anti-Semitic Houston Stewart Chamberlain, who believed in the existence of a pure Aryan race. The most hideous historical expression of these racialist views was the anti-Semitism of German Fascism, which asserted that the 'blood' of the Jews defiled the supposedly pure and superior Aryan race. Such racialist views about the 'natural' divisions of humanity into permanent physical types have been shown to have no scientific basis whatsoever, as genetic variability may be greater within a race than between races. These views have, deservedly, been rejected today by all serious analysts.

Culture as an explanation

However, the scholarly rejection of these racialist views has not put an end to considerations about the divisions of humanity. Clearly, these divisions still exist, and it is necessary to consider why this should be. The late 19th- and early 20th-century historian Heinrich von Treitschke, a German nationalist of little restraint, thought that the antagonism between races was of little relevance to the national divisions of humanity into states. Instead, Treitschke, in this regard like the Frenchman Ernest Renan, thought that the existence of separate nations was not a matter of biology, but of history. This view indicates that the divisions of humanity are a consequence of human invention, that is, cultural, and, hence, not 'given' in nature. This was also the view of the influential 18th-century writer on the divisions of humanity, Johann Gottfried von Herder.

An interesting argument for the division of humanity that focused on cultural factors was offered before and after World War II by the scholar of Indo-European religions, Georges Dumézil. He argued that there was a culture that was unique to a supposedly common Indo-European character. According to Dumézil, the structure of the Indo-European culture had three levels, each of which had a specific function. The function of the first level was that of ruling and the administration of the sacred, represented by king and priest. The function of the second level was that of force, represented by the warrior. The third was that of production, represented by cultivators and labourers. He further argued that this Indo-European culture was uniquely embodied in and expressed by the Indo-European languages. As a consequence, he thought that this culture was necessarily different from those of other language groups.

Dumézil's argument is relevant for this investigation because the members of a nation often view language as an important factor in distinguishing their nation from another. This perspective of a cultural inheritance, shared, albeit with differences, by Herder, Renan, and Treitschke, rejects a belief in the biologically given (which is now assumed to be universal to the human species) in favour of a recognition of the 'givenness' of the cultural divisions of humanity, whether by civilization or by nation. Nevertheless, the existence of such cultural divisions poses a number of problems. How flexible are they? Above all, how is one to understand humanity's tendency to differentiate itself into societies, each of which has its own cultural heritage and a language that bears that heritage?

These questions point to problems that underlie the current

controversy about the so-called 'clash of civilizations', each with its own distinctive cultural heritage, for example between Judaeo-Christian, Islamic, and Confucian, where Dumézil's structuralist argument might account for historically deep-seated differences between various linguistic groups of peoples, whether civilizations or nations. However, the apparent linguistic and institutional similarities that Dumézil thought were common to a number of early Indo-European societies and their mythologies, and which seem to distinguish those societies from those of other language groups, or even civilizations, might be neither distinctive nor inflexible. The distinctiveness of those institutional forms he attributed to the early Indo-Europeans could be a consequence of similar stages in social development rather than a common linguistic origin. Moreover, the cultural structure of three levels may be a consequence of the requirements necessary for any society to exist – specifically, the need for order (including a justification for that order); the need for protection from external threats; and the provision of goods required to sustain life. If this is so, then the supposed distinctiveness that separates one culture from another is either exaggerated or, given further historical development, will undergo modification. Perhaps increased international trade and beliefs such as those in human rights will undermine the divisions between one nation or civilization from another.

Nonetheless, even those who wish humanity well must be sceptical about the extent to which such developments will undermine human divisiveness. This is so because, so far, cultural developments like the universal monotheistic religions, international trade, and communication that spans the globe have by no means undermined the divisions within humanity. Moreover, these cultural developments have not even undermined deep divisions, national or otherwise, within a particular civilization. This is obvious from the all too numerous events of the 20th century: for the Judaeo-Christian civilization, two World Wars and Fascism; for the civilizations of the East, the racialist militarism of the Japanese, militant Hinduism, and the military clashes between

China and Vietnam; and for Islamic civilization, the war between Iran and Iraq.

Certainly, the universal, monotheistic religions have in the past undermined previously existing, localized groups through the creation of extensive communities of faith; but they have often done so by subsequently contributing to the consolidation of these local groups into nations. For example, contributing to the consolidation of the Franks of early medieval Europe into a nation was their belief that they were a people uniquely chosen by God to defend Christianity; and defend it they did, against their fellow Christians. Likewise, the Armenians from the 4th to the 8th centuries CE were consolidated into a nation by their adoption of Christianity. Examples of universal religions contributing to the consolidation of nations are, as was observed in the previous chapter, to be found from other civilizations: the Sinhalese from the 5th century CE understood themselves to be the Buddhist nation of Sri Lanka in opposition to Hinduism (and the Tamils); and the further consolidation of Iran during the 16th century CE into a nation was abetted by the belief that it was Shi'ite, in opposition to the Sunni beliefs of the Ottomans.

Thus, the relation between seemingly universal developments, such as the monotheistic religions and international trade, and the limiting traditions of territorial kinship turns out to be complicated, because such traditions may persist despite these developments. Consider, for example, the resilience of those beliefs in some kind of uniqueness of a nation that are expressed in recent movements of what is called 'regionalism'. These 'proto-national' movements appear not only in relatively less technologically advanced areas of Asia, for example Kashmir, but also in more economically advanced areas that have been the primary channels for modern life, with its emphasis on the belief in the rights of the individual for all of humanity, for example Quebec, Scotland, and Euzkadi. If only such divisions were phenomena of the past, soon to be swept away by the influence of international trade! The facts indicate otherwise.

To recognize that the assumed 'givenness' of the nation that is thought to distinguish one nation from another may be a consequence of any number of historical factors only raises other problems. While the historical foundation of these distinctions may be an indication of the inventiveness of the human imagination, such that nations or any number of other human relationships are not biologically given (and the wide variability, both by scope and by purpose, of these relationships suggests as much), how are we to understand this capacity for invention? Moreover, why should different cultural traditions exist at all? Why do they appear so prevalent and persistent throughout history? And why have they been repeatedly expressed through terms of kinship? Is it possible that while mankind is an inventive species and, as such, the relations it forms are 'artificial', nevertheless, those relations are not arbitrary? If they aren't arbitrary, do humans form nations out of necessity, or even a biological tendency towards divisiveness?

The biology of 'us' versus 'them'

Various biological explanations have been put forth for the existence and tenacity of the cultural divisions of humanity into distinct groupings, of which the nation is one. One explanation has been economic competition; namely, that the scarcity of resources to satisfy ever-expanding and seemingly often conflicting human desires (including not only those of immediate physical satisfaction, such as hunger, but also more complex aims like prestige) has resulted in humans banding together into groups, which, in turn, compete with one another for those resources. This explanation rests, however indirectly, on a particular understanding of human biology, as does another explanation for the existence of the state made famous by Thomas Hobbes; namely, the calculation to come together so that the life of the individual may be made more secure. These explanations are attempts to clarify, in the idiom of evolutionary biology, strategies of adaptation for the preservation of life.

Some neo-Darwinians and evolutionary psychologists have explained the formation of competing groups as an adaptive response of 'inclusive fitness'; that is, to further the transmission of one's genes and those of your kin in the face of scarcity and any number of threats, such as predators or strangers, to that transmission. If, in fact, humans are 'evolutionarily programmed' to increase the likelihood of the transmission of their own genes, then, so the argument goes, cooperation both to secure limited, contested resources and for protection, initially in support of one's family (an expression of genetic favouritism), would have required the formation of various forms of larger groups. These groups are understood by their members in terms of kinship because such an understanding would then serve to extend the inclusive fitness of genetic transmission to those with whom one cooperates. Thus, the beliefs around which various forms of kinship are formed are historically so persistent because they are, in some way, derivative of and facilitate the biologically given.

The temptation facing the Darwinian is to provide a biological account for all of human behaviour, because ultimately, as for all naturalistic accounts of human behaviour, no contrast exists between nature and culture, as the latter must serve the former. Thus, for such biological explanations of human conduct, the existence of distinct and competing groups of varying kinds must serve some adaptive purpose, because otherwise they would not exist.

There is likely some merit to incorporating biological facts into the social and historical sciences. However, here, too, problems arise. First, there is the ambiguity of what it means to be 'evolutionarily programmed'. When one considers that women who earn a college degree are 50% more likely than other women to be childless, or that populations of nations with a high standard of living have fewer children, to the point of exhibiting zero population growth or even declining populations, one wonders what it means to be 'evolutionarily programmed' for genetic self-interest. Why, when scarcity and other threats to one's existence have been minimized, should some people, both individually or as a national aggregate, choose not to have children; and thereby seemingly undermine 'inclusive fitness'? Second, there is the difficulty in accounting for, in biological terms, the belief in being genetically related to those for whom this is factually not so. Furthermore, while the cultural formation of a kinship group significantly larger than the family may provide a structure for efficient cooperation in the pursuit and allocation of resources through the formulation of criteria – cultural markers such as language – indicating who can and cannot be trusted, is such a formation ultimately adaptive or maladaptive? How is one to explain kinds of conduct that appear to contradict the statement of initial conditions of furthering genetic transmission, such as the suicidal struggle for national prestige, or wars of mass destruction between nations?

Some Darwinians might respond that these examples are expressions of maladaption arising from the fact that humans have stone-age minds in modern skulls; that is, the adaptive mechanisms of natural and sexual selection necessarily lag behind the rapidly changing cultural environment. However, such a response is an admission that at any particular point there may be no direct relation between nature and many cultural expressions of human conduct; or if there must be such a relation, we today are not in a position to say what it is, as we lack the perspective of many millennia to make such a determination.

The diversity of human behaviour

The complicating factor for naturalistic accounts of human behaviour is that culture is not uniform. Humans engage in a multitude of diverse activities in pursuit of incomparable, indeed at times contradictory goals, for example a tendency to form distinct and competing groups such as nations along with a tendency to assert the unity of humanity, as in the monotheistic religions. What is at issue here comes down to this: how is one to understand the evident human ability to make a choice between different and seemingly incomparable alternatives, such as going to war for one's country or refusing to kill a fellow human being? Does the existence of such alternatives and the ability to choose between them indicate an 'openness of the mind to the world', or 'freedom'? The behaviourist who thinks that human conduct is determined by biological drives may object to such a possibility by insisting that 'choice' is merely a consequence of either the lag of evolutionary adaptation or the excessive cost of information to maximize efficiently one's pleasure or preference. Such objections, however, have the appearance of 'just so' stories in the service of maintaining the exclusivity of the explanatory mechanism of the asserted initial condition, in this case behaviourally determining biological drives.

To recognize a diversity of human goals does not invalidate the merit of either Darwinian or economic accounts of human behaviour, for the different pursuits of humanity, their associated social organizations (for example, nation and church), and the ability to choose between them surely have biological foundations. However, it restricts their explanatory merit. The question that accords better to the facts of human behaviour is how to understand diverse, even contradictory, human purposes. These observations lead to a consideration of the relation between the diverse ways humanity organizes itself and the biological imperatives, or behaviourism, of the animal kingdom. It is the problem of clarifying the ambiguity of the 'givenness' of human division, of which the nation is one example. The goal here will be modest: to outline various difficulties involved in clarifying this ambiguity, thereby indicating complications rather than providing definitive answers. Some observations by Aristotle will be useful in focusing our attention on these difficulties.

Aristotle observed that humans were animals because of their biological drive to reproduce and preserve themselves. However, he also observed that there were other traits that distinguished humans from the rest of the animal kingdom, specifically the capacity for speech. While there is evidence that non-human primates communicate, they certainly do not exhibit the capacity to do so to the degree that humans do. Of course, even if one locates traits that distinguish humans from the rest of the animal kingdom, their existence has antecedents in the animal kingdom. Certainly, the theorists of evolutionary biology are right to pursue those antecedents by postulating probable adaptations of the developing human form to the environments of hundreds of thousands, even millions, of years ago during the Plio-Pleistocene era that have made those traits possible. These adaptations include upright posture; the opposable thumb that facilitates the fashioning of tools; an enlarged, complex brain, which grows significantly after birth; the paradoxical combination of being both an isolated individual and involved with others, entailing one's desire both to conceal oneself from others (which includes self-deception) and to reveal oneself to others through the expectation of recognition and approval; and instincts that do not thoroughly determine behaviour, thus the likely associated 'openness of the mind' to new environments, including those created by humans that, once created, provide various foci of attention – structures of tradition – to which human conduct is oriented. To reformulate our problem: to what extent are these various environments of human creation, of which the nation is one, 'given'?

Aristotle also observed that humans have the ability to 'foresee with the mind'. This orientation to the future results in humans organizing themselves into seemingly qualitatively different forms of social relations in the attempt to address different problems, including those problems that are in the process of being created. Thus, Aristotle thought that the household and the city are distinguished from one another according to different purposes in response to different problems: for the family, the biological problem of the generation and sustenance of life itself; for the city, the cultural problem of not just living, but how best to live, of living well. This recognition of seemingly qualitatively different problems that, in turn, elicit different orientations of behaviour was shared by

Adam Smith, when, in the *Theory of Moral Sentiments*, he drew attention to the human distinction between what is useful and what is proper.

Does humanity's introduction of the problem of what is proper – the problem of the meaning of existence – that leads to the formation of diverse, indeed at times conflicting, social organizations (family, city, nation, empire, universal church, and so forth) indicate that there is only an indirect relation between those organizations and humanity's biological constitution? Even at the level of kinship, the variability of its forms, indicating that the concept refers to more than one object (ranging from the biological tie between mother and child to a relatedness of territorial cohabitation and even to speaking a common language), has led many analysts to insist on only an indirect relation between various social relations created by man and biology. If this is the case, then the explanatory merit of the relation between social relations such as the nation and biology is limited. Instead, the problem confronting the analyst is to examine various traditions of conduct, their institutional expression, the modifications both undergo over time, and the relation of one tradition to another. Thus, the ambiguity of the belief in the givenness of the nation is clarified through the recognition of a wide-ranging malleability of human conduct, even if that malleability is a consequence of biological properties that have evolutionarily emerged over time. Still, the problem remains as to how to understand the historical persistence of the social relation of kinship, albeit a social relation that has taken different forms.

Let us retrace some of the steps of the argument. This is the puzzle facing those who wish to understand the nation: humanity is part of the animal kingdom, yet in some ways distinguished from the rest of it. How so? Specific to humanity is the capacity to divide oneself into subject and object, to think about oneself, to reflect upon one's own condition; and, thereby, not only to engage in a struggle for existence, but also to raise the problem of what is the proper way to live. This is the capacity for self-consciousness. However, this capacity for self-reflection (the 'openness of the mind to the world', including a world that is internal to the individual) bears with it an awareness of humanity's deficiencies – above all, suffering and death – in relation to both its current and future environment. In Western civilization, the classic formulation of the ordeal of the self-awareness of this deficiency is 'the opening of the eyes' of Adam and Eve and the subsequent discovery of their nakedness, with its resultant shame, as described in Genesis 3.

In response to this openness and the anxiety that it provokes, the mind seeks out and establishes varieties of order that provide structure to experience. These varieties of order – traditions – are expressed in different forms of relations. These, in turn, are formed around different meanings about life that arise out of the contemplation of experience. Thus, in response to a meaning of life focused on its generation and transmission, relations of kinship such as family, clan, and nation are formed; a meaning of life revolving around freedom is expressed in varying political relations of self-government, such as democracy; and a preoccupation with the suffering of life and the release from it manifests itself in different religious traditions and their organization through churches.

There may be biological traits to the formation of these relations and the traditions around which they are constituted, for example the minimization of anxiety – or strategies of adaptation, as it would be formulated in evolutionary biology – arising out of the awareness of the perceived deficiencies or uncertainties of our existence. Perhaps the social relations formed in response to this self-awareness are the human equivalent of the biologically given instincts that dominate the behaviour of the rest of the animal kingdom. In other words, in contrast to the developed instinctual apparatus found in the animal kingdom that so thoroughly determines activity (including where one animal co-exists with another, like bees in a beehive) humans create wide-ranging social relations that structure their conduct, thereby reducing the anxiety of the uncertainty of how to act arising from the lack of such a behaviourally determining instinctual apparatus.

These conduct-structuring social relations provide patterns of familiarity; and they, too, are inherited – to be sure, not genetically, but through a cultural heritage. The consequence of the development of the human mind after birth is that it is 'open' (or, as formulated in the idiom of evolutionary psychology and cognitive science, the brain's processing module is not dominated by a specific instinct) to a particular cultural heritage. For example, the developing mind of the child learns the language and other traditions of the society in which the child is raised. As such, a cultural inheritance becomes a part of the image that one forms of oneself, thereby rooting in the psyche and habit of the individual the familiarity provided by the culture into which the individual is born and develops. The primary vehicle for this cultural inheritance is language; that is, to acquire a language is to acquire its content, as Dumézil observed. Furthermore, those who are recognized as speaking a common language are also recognized as sharing in that familiarity. Perhaps this individually inherited familiarity and its biological importance in reducing anxiety goes some way in accounting for the persistence of the belief in being related that is characteristic of the nation. It seems likely that part of the significance of the nation is that it is a structure of familiarity. If so, it becomes clear why a common language is often understood to be one of the characteristic factors of the nation; and why the preservation of that language, as the bearer of a unique cultural inheritance, is so important to the members of the nation.

Despite the likelihood of this behavioural component to a cultural heritage, humans can adopt a critical stance to such an inheritance by raising the problem of what is the proper way to live. If there is indeed some behavioural element to the formation of social relations, including the nation (and, as humans are part of the animal kingdom, how could there not be?), the human capacity for self-reflection breaks into what would otherwise be the deterministic relationship between the person and his or her environment, including the inherited cultural environment. Thus, the relations between the individual and the environment, and between one individual and another, become subject to contemplation and evaluation. Let us consider as an example the uniting of man and woman for the purpose of procreation.

Whatever the degree of biological instinct operating in the drive of humans to procreate and to form relations for procreation, that instinct is subject to reflection. Because humans subject the biological drive to procreate to evaluation, it becomes susceptible to variability, as expressed in the many different forms of human mating – not only monogamy, but also polygamy, promiscuity (for example, prostitution, adultery), and separation of the male and female after mating (as in divorce). Such variability, even when confined to biologically compelling sexual relations, within a species is characteristically human. Indeed, humans may reject altogether both what may otherwise be understood as a behavioural drive to procreate and the social relations derivative of that drive, the family. Such a decision arises from orienting one's actions out of consideration of a different understanding of what it means to live properly, as one finds expressed, for example, in Matthew 19:12, 'and there are eunuchs who have made themselves eunuchs for the sake of the kingdom of heaven'.

Different social relations

There are other abilities that distinguish humans from other primates. Human natural habitats do not seem to be natural; that is, humans exhibit the capacity to adapt to diverse environments. Furthermore, humans are capable of forming relations beyond any of these diverse, immediately given environments; that is, beyond the spatial area of the behavioural mechanisms of smell, touch, and sight, and out of a consideration beyond the temporal horizon of what is present. This capability is evident from those human relations such as trade for goods over long distances, and those many religions for which an event in the distant past, for example the crucifixion of Jesus, is seen as relevant for one's conduct in the present. This capability is also evident in the creation of the nation, the territorial expansiveness of which is beyond the spatial area of the smell, touch, and sight of any one individual, although pictorial representations, maps, of the nation imaginatively extend one's vision. The ability to form such relations indicates that the human mind exhibits capacities of imagination that enable it to lay claim to spatially distant locations as being in some way one's own, to lay claim to events in the past as relevant to one's present, to lay claim to a vision of the future as a concern of that present, and to lay claim to the images of a past, present, and future of another individual as being one's own. Various relations may be differentiated from one another – and we seek the ways that are specific to the nation – by the variability of the above-mentioned criteria of space and time; but there is another differentiating criterion, the purpose of the relation.

When images about things in the past, present, or expected in the future held in the mind of one individual are shared by another, they become the criteria by which individuals may evaluate one another. Those images held by one individual about another posit qualities – that may or may not be physically real – about that other individual. The result of such an evaluative classification is that one individual is recognized to be in some way either similar to another, such that a 'we' is established, or different from another such that an 'other' is asserted. Examples of the formation of a 'we' are the nation, where the quality recognized is the location of birth; and Christianity, in which what is recognized is the belief in Jesus Christ as Lord and Saviour. The degree of such similarity or difference varies depending upon the criteria recognized and asserted about the other individual; it varies according to the purpose of the relation that, in turn, influences the choice and significance, or lack thereof, of those evaluative criteria.

The relation of a recognized commonality, or lack thereof, may be temporally episodic, for example when a grain producer enters into a contract with a buyer. There are temporal elements to this kind of relationship because the decision of the producer of grain to enter into a contractual relationship with the buyer is based on both past experience and the future expectation of a profit. There are also spatial elements to this relationship. The contracting parties may be 'face to face' with each other, for example in a village market; or they may be spatially distant from one another such that they never meet, for example in international trade. If the 'we' of such a contractual relationship entered into out of the purpose of an expected advantage to each of the individuals is not established, then there may exist the condition of 'otherness' between what then becomes two competitors. Such a relationship is temporally episodic because it endures only as long as the contract is specified.

Characteristic of this economic relationship of an exchange of goods and services of the modern, spatially extensive market place is an impersonality between the contracting individuals. In this example of the contract, ideally, one individual of the contractual relationship either suspends or ignores altogether many of the qualities that he or she perceives about the other individual with whom the contract is entered into, as each pursues their own advantage, except for the expectation (entailing trust) that both parties to the contract will honestly fulfil their part of the contract. Thus, for efficient economic relations, national or religious properties asserting the similarity or dissimilarity of one individual as perceived by another should be irrelevant as criteria for entering into a contractual exchange of goods and services. Such an impersonality of the ideal economic relationship presupposes a degree of toleration in so far as those other evaluative criteria are either suspended or viewed as irrelevant for the purpose of this kind of relationship. Free trade, as the economist and philosopher Frank Knight noted, enshrines the doctrine of 'live and let live'.

The character of the relation of the religious organization is temporally more enduring than that of the economic exchange of the market because, in contrast to the latter, it introduces evaluative criteria that assert something fundamental about the existence of the individual. In this case, a relationship of similarity between two worshippers is asserted based on their shared recognition of both a past event that determines their present condition, for example one of sinfulness, and an expected event that will determine their future condition, for example salvation. Those who do not share that image of both past and future conditions, and who, thus, do not order their actions accordingly, are outside the religious organization. Those recognized to be outsiders might be believed by the members of the organization to be condemned to eternal perdition. In the character of the religious organization, certain evaluative criteria that indicate the purpose of the association such as, for Christianity, the recognition of Jesus as Lord and Saviour, or, for Islam, the recognition of Muhammad as the final true prophet, are not ignored; they, instead, define the relationship. In these examples of Christianity and Islam, spatial criteria do not play such an important role in the evaluation of one individual by another.

Turning to the nation, there is a significant evaluative component such that the qualities perceived in one individual by another and vice versa usually, except for the legal process of 'naturalization', define both individuals for their entire lives. The significance of the evaluative criteria that humans employ such that nations exist – criteria that assert divisions within humanity – is to be distinguished from the absence or suspension of that significance when humans enter into economic relationships, in which, at least ideally, there is a toleration of one another. It is also to be distinguished from Christianity, Islam, and Buddhism, in which, at least doctrinally, criteria are recognized that reject national divisions of humanity as they assert universal brotherhood.

The world religions are religions of belief. One can become a Christian, Muslim, or Buddhist by accepting their respective doctrines. In contrast, the quality recognized in a fellow member of a nation centres on birth, usually birth in its territory. This focus, resulting in relations of kinship ranging from the family to the nation, limits the potential for the expansiveness of the social relation. Nevertheless, various historical factors – law, politics, communication, and religion – can expand the relation of kinship through the creation of a common, territorially expansive culture. The 'we' of the territorial community of the nation is larger than the territorial communities of a clan, tribe, or city-state. Thus, expansion of the territorial relations of kinship is clearly possible. Perhaps one day the evaluative and distinguishing significance attributed to where one is born will fade from human consciousness; but it has not happened yet. Moreover, other considerations intervene to limit the extent of such an expansion, for example the desire for the freedom of self-government. Whatever the reasons, the division of humanity into nations continues.

Chapter 8
Conclusion

At the beginning of this millennium, nations remain one of the ways by which humanity has organized, and thereby divided and evaluated, itself. In addition, the uncivil ideology of nationalism continues, often tragically, to have a hold, with varying degrees of intensity, on the imagination of humanity. One consequence of such nationalistic enchantment – for example, the murder of innocent civilians in the Balkans, in Kashmir, or in Kurdistan by those who are intoxicated by an ideal that permits no compromise – is the destruction of the prospect of delight in the everyday pleasures of life, just as Homer described the danger of the Sirens for Odysseus and his crew in *The Odyssey*. The use of Homer's description of the destructive potential of an all-encompassing enchantment to describe the danger of the ideology of nationalism suggests that in some ways the problems that confront humanity have over the millennia changed less than one might think. Indeed, the intention of this book is to clarify what the approximately 3,000-year-old story of the Tower of Babel purports to explain about one of these problems: the division of humanity into distinct nations, each of which is formed around beliefs in its own territory, language, and supposedly unique biological kinship. These features, thought to distinguish one group of humans from another, are also found in the tenth chapter of Genesis, where the biblical Hebrew *gôy* is translated in most English versions of the Bible as 'nation'.

Scholarly examinations about the division of humanity into nations began to appear in the latter half of the 18th century, and by the 20th century the number of such works had grown significantly. There were several reasons for this increased scholarly attention. One was the attempt to come to terms with the brutality of World War I, during which millions of people were killed in the mass mobilization of one nation against another, naively believed at that time to have put an end to all war. Other reasons were the doctrine of the principle of national self-determination as put forward in 1918 by Woodrow Wilson, then President of the United States of America, in response to the dismemberment of the Austro-Hungarian and Ottoman Empires, and the institution of the League of Nations that arose in the aftermath of that war.

Further reasons for the appearance of works on the nation and the ideology of nationalism soon arose: Italian and German Fascism; World War II; and the emergence of political movements in Asia and Africa whose goal, in the name of national self-determination, was to rid those areas of European presence. The appearance of Fascism required a refinement of analysis, indicating the necessity to distinguish both uncivil nationalism as an ideology, and the even more grotesque manifestation of this ideology as Fascism, from the nation. Finally, the political movements in the aftermath of World War II for national self-determination revealed clearly the drive of a nation to be free to determine its own affairs through its organization as an independent national state.

There were always theoretical disputes surrounding the concept of the nation. These disputes, without too much oversimplification, can be reduced to two. First, there is the problem of the degree to which a national culture (the nature of which has also been a matter of disagreement) is a factor in the formation of the character of an individual. An individual can understand himself or herself in different ways, for example as a member of a family, a nation, or a world religion. How important is the self-understanding of being a member of a nation, and why does it sometimes dominate other understandings of the self?

The second dispute concerns the extent to which the appearance of nations is to be viewed as historically recent. Many economists, political scientists, and sociologists think that the belief in political equality of individuals (expressed in democracy and modern forms of citizenship), industrial capitalism (requiring a territorially large and culturally uniform population), and modern means of communication brought about the existence of nations. They characterize these political and economic developments as 'modernization'. I have presented evidence in this book that casts doubt on the merit of this argument that nations are historically novel. Furthermore, there arose predictions that, as a result of modernization, for example the ever-increasing international division of labour and entities such as the European Union, nations would soon disappear.

Now, however, events have taken place that heighten these disputes and create others. In contrast to predictions of the disappearance of nations, what emerged from the collapse of the Soviet Union and the reunification of Germany only made evident the persistence of national attachments in the face of modernization and an increasing international division of labour. During the last twenty years, this persistence has at times been expressed passionately, tragically so, as in the Balkans, where, once again, the enchanting Siren of nationalism bewitched those who made certain that not only their victims but they, too, would not enjoy the everyday delights of life. Moreover, confounding earlier analyses of modernization, within such engines of modern life as North America and the United Kingdom there arose national or regional movements of separation, respectively Quebec and Scotland. These and other events, such as the continuing conflict between India and Pakistan, ethnic warfare in Africa, and the continuing significance of religion as a factor in these circumstances, indicated the persistence and resilience of national attachments in the face of doctrines (obviously, but not only, including socialism) that were explicitly anti-national. Some socialists recognized this persistence and modified their views accordingly. The significance of this persistence requires explanation, especially as it complicates the scholarly orthodoxy of the day, namely, the understanding of human action that is excessively individualistic and utilitarian. The nation has, now more than ever, become a thorn in the side of rational man.

The events of the 20th century are of pressing importance for those who wish to understand nations and nationalism. Interpretations of these events, and discussions of the theoretical disputes that they aroused – for example, whether or not nations are modern, or the nature of the attachments the individual forms to the image of the nation and to other individuals who share that image – are currently the key issues being discussed in academic circles. However, the justification for this book on nationalism exists beyond one more discussion of those disputes. I have, instead, pursued a problem that, while related to those disputes, is nevertheless of a different orientation. The focus of this book was an investigation of the question, what does the existence of nations say about human beings? The pursuit of this question does not mean that those scholarly disputes, of which I have been a participant, were ignored; but they were not at the centre of the argument.

In the attempt to answer this problem, we must also speculate on why nations exist. Too often scholars eschew such an orientation because they wish to avoid any element of speculation. By refusing to enter into a discussion of what nations might tell us about the nature of humanity, those scholars wrongly avoid the problem of why the nation is of such interest and pressing concern to humanity.

One reason for the persistence and importance of nations, offered in the previous chapters, is that humans are preoccupied with vitality, above all, its origins. As a consequence of this preoccupation, they form relations around those origins, of which the most obvious example is the family, centred around the mother and father as the source of life. It is likely that such a preoccupation accounts for the persistence of the formation, albeit historically variable, of different structures of kinship. The complication posed by the nation to the formation of structures of kinship is that it introduces an extensive, yet bounded territory as a further element in this preoccupation with vitality. The significance of birth, for the formation of both the family and the nation, must be pondered. Parents put the well-being of their children before their own; members of a nation may sacrifice their lives for the well-being of their nation; and it is such self-sacrifice, so frequent throughout the 20th century, which requires acknowledgement.

However, this is not the only meaning around which humans organize themselves. There are relations that transcend the preoccupation with vitality, as they are concerned with the proper way to live. In religious categories, the contrast between these two relations is one between paganism and monotheism, both of which appear to be persistent in human affairs.

The task of politics is not to repudiate these different orientations of human conduct. To champion uncompromisingly one of those orientations at the expense of the other only invites a totalitarian enchantment with one of their ideological expressions, whether nationalism or fundamentalism. The task of politics, through the reasoned exercise of the virtue of civility arising out of concern for the unavoidably ambiguous common good of one's society, is to adjudicate artfully between the demands that these orientations place on human life.

References

Chapter 1

For an example of the term 'Sumerian seed', see the 'Letter from Ibbi-Sin to Puzur-Numushda' in Samuel Noah Kramer, *The Sumerians* (Chicago, 1963).

For the ancient Egyptian contrast to the Nubians and 'Asiatics', see A. Kirk Grayson and Donald B. Redford (eds.), *Papyrus and Tablet* (Englewood, NJ, 1973), p. 22; and John A. Wilson, *The Burden of Egypt* (Chicago, 1951), p. 164.

Herodotus, *The History*, tr. David Grene (Chicago, 1987), Bk. 8.144.

For the Chinese characterization of the *Di* and *Rohn*, see Michael Loewe and Edward L. Shaughnessy (eds.), *The Cambridge History of Ancient China* (Cambridge, 1999).

For the contempt implied by *bárbaros*, see Frank Walbank, 'The Problem of Greek Nationality', in *Selected Papers* (Cambridge, 1985).

Plato, *The Republic*, tr. Allan Bloom (New York, 1968), Bk. 5, 469a–471b; see also *The Menexenus*, tr. B. Jowett, *The Collected Dialogues of Plato*, ed. Edith Hamilton and Huntington Cairns (Princeton, 1961), 245d.

For the existence of pre-modern nations, see Steven Grosby, *Biblical Ideas of Nationality: Ancient and Modern* (Winona Lake, IN, 2002); Anthony D. Smith, *The Antiquity of Nations* (Cambridge, 2004).

Chapter 2

For vitality and the nation, see Steven Grosby, 'Primordiality' in *Encyclopaedia of Nationalism*, ed. Athena S. Leoussi (New Brunswick, 2001); Donald L. Horowitz, 'The Primordialists' in *Ethnonationalism in the Contemporary World*, ed. Daniele Conversi (London, 2002); Anthony D. Smith, *Nationalism and Modernism* (London, 1998).

Anthony D. Smith, *The Ethnic Origin of Nations* (Oxford, 1986).

Adam Smith, *The Theory of Moral Sentiments*, eds. D. D. Raphael and A. L. Macfie (Indianapolis, 1982), p. 192.

Aristotle, *The Politics*, tr. Carnes Lord (Chicago, 1984), 1252a1.

For civility as a mode of conduct, see *The Virtue of Civility: Selected Essays of Edward Shils on Liberalism, Tradition, and Civil Society*, ed. Steven Grosby (Indianapolis, 1997); Michael Oakeshott, *On Human Conduct* (Oxford, 1975).

For Cato the Elder, see Plutarch, *The Lives of the Noble Grecians and Romans*, tr. John Dryden (New York, nd).

On the nation as a medium between the empire and anarchy, see Yoram Hazony, 'The Case for the National State', *Azure* 12: 27–70.

Ernest Renan, 'What is a Nation?' in *The Poetry of the Celtic Races and Other Studies* (London, 1896).

On the dual nature of the nation, see Dominique Schnapper, *Community of Citizens*, tr. Séverine Rosée (New Brunswick, 1998).

For the defining characteristics of a nation, see Anthony D. Smith, 'When is a Nation?', *Geopolitics* 7/2 (2002): 5–32; *The Antiquity of Nations* (Cambridge, 2004), pp. 16–19.

Chapter 3

For the distinction between social relation and tool, see Hans Freyer, *Theory of Objective Mind: An Introduction to the Philosophy of Culture*, tr. Steven Grosby (Athens, 1998).

For the invention of tradition, see Eric Hobsbawm, 'Introduction: Inventing Traditions' in *The Invention of Tradition*, ed. Eric Hobsbawm and Terence Ranger (Cambridge, 1983).

For the history of the tartan kilt, see Hugh Trevor-Roper, 'The Invention of Tradition: The Highland Tradition of Scotland' in *The Invention of Tradition*, ed. Eric Hobsbawm and Terence Ranger (Cambridge, 1983).

On the relation of the Dutch to the Batavians, see Simon Schama, *The Embarrassment of Riches: An Interpretation of Dutch Culture in the Golden Age* (New York, 1987).

On emigration, immigration, and the civic-ethnic distinction, see Patrick Weil, 'Access to Citizenship' in *Citizenship Today*, ed. T. Alexander Aleinikoff and Douglas Klusmeyer (Washington, DC, 2001).

On the *hiyal*, see Joseph Schacht, 'The Law' in *Unity and Variety in Muslim Civilization*, ed. Gustave E. von Grunebaum (Chicago, 1955); Abraham L. Udovitch, *Partnership and Profit in Medieval Islam* (New Haven, 1979).

R. C. van Caenegem, *Legal History* (London, 1991), p. 119.

On the vassal and the ambiguities of the category feudalism, see Susan Reynolds, *Fiefs and Vassals* (Oxford, 1994).

On the legal developments in England during the 12th to 13th centuries, still indispensable are Frederick Pollock and Frederic William Maitland, *The History of English Law before the Time of Edward I* (Cambridge, 1923); Maitland's *The Constitutional History of England* (Cambridge, 1920); and William Stubbs, *The Constitutional History of England* (Chicago, 1979).

For this definition of the jury, see Frederick Pollock and Frederic William Maitland, *The History of English Law*, vol. 1, p. 138.

On the contribution of the medieval army and the longbow to the development of the English nation, see Barnaby C. Keeney, 'Military Service and the Development of Nationalism in England, 1272–1327', *Speculum* XXII/4 (October 1947): 534–49.

Fritz Kern, Kingship and Law in the Middle Ages (Oxford, 1939).

Chapter 4

For these ancient Near Eastern tribes, see M. B. Rowton, 'Enclosed Nomadism', *Journal of the Economic and Social History of the Orient* 17 (1974): 1–30; 'Dimorphic Structure and the Parasocial Element', *Journal of Near Eastern Studies* 36 (1977): 181–98.

On the historical ubiquity of the territorial tie, see Robert Lowie, *The State* (New York, 1927).

On *gayum*, see Abraham Malamat, *Mari and the Early Israelite Experience* (Oxford, 1989).

Plato, *The Menexenus*, tr. B. Jowett, *The Collected Dialogues of Plato*, ed. Edith Hamilton and Huntington Cairns (Princeton, 1961), 237b–238b.

On the influence of the ancient Israelite conception of the promised land for the formation of nations in European history, see Adrian Hastings, *The Construction of Nationhood* (Cambridge, 1997).

Lyndon Baines Johnson, *A Time for Action* (New York, 1964).

For temples as boundary markers for the ancient Greek city-states, see François de Polignac, *Cults, Territory and the Origins of the Greek City-State* (Chicago, 1995).

John Locke, *Second Treatise of Government*, ed. Peter Laslett (Cambridge, 1960), ch. v.

Ernest Renan, 'What is a Nation?' in *The Poetry of the Celtic Races and Other Studies* (London, 1896).

Chapter 5

For analyses of nationality as exclusively modern, see, for example, Ernest Gellner, *Nations and Nationalism* (Ithaca, 1983); E. J. Hobsbawm, *Nations and Nationalism since 1780* (Cambridge, 1990); Liah Greenfeld, *Nationalism: Five Roads to Modernity* (Cambridge 1992).

On early Sinhalese history, see Bardwell L. Smith (ed.), *Religion and Legitimation of Power in Sri Lanka* (Chambersburg, 1978); K. M. de Silva, *A History of Sri Lanka* (Berkeley, 1981).

On nationality in ancient Israelite history, see Steven Grosby, *Biblical Ideas of Nationality; Ancient and Modern* (Winona Lake, IN, 2002).

On early Japanese history, see Delmer M. Brown (ed.), *The Cambridge History of Japan*, vol. 1 (Cambridge, 1993); Joseph Kitagawa, 'The Japanese *Kokutai* (National Community): History and Myth', *History of Religions* 13/3 (1974): 209–26.

On medieval Polish history, see Paul W. Knoll, *The Rise of the Polish Monarchy* (Chicago, 1972); Norman Davies, *God's Playground*, vol. 1 (New York, 1982).

Delmer M. Brown, 'The Early Evolution of Historical Consciousness' in *The Cambridge History of Japan*, vol. 1, p. 506.

On European trans-national institutions and human rights, see David Jacobson, *Rights Across Borders* (Baltimore, 1996).

On the possibility of Levites as government officials, see G. W. Ahlström, *Royal Administration and National Religion in Ancient Palestine* (Leiden, 1982).

On these samurai's slogans and an overview of Tokugawa Japan, see E. H. Norman, *Origins of the Modern Japanese State* (New York, 1975); W. G. Beasley, *The Japanese Experience* (Berkeley, 1999).

On the account of the pronunciation of Polish words, see Paul W. Knoll, *The Rise of the Polish Monarchy*, p. 33; Norman Davies, *God's Playground*, p. 94.

Josephus, *The Antiquities of the Jews*, in *The Works of Josephus*, tr. William Whiston (Peabody, MA, 1987), 13.9.1.

For these characteristics of nationality, see Anthony D. Smith, 'When is a Nation?', *Geopolitics* 7/2 (2002): 5–32; *The Antiquity of Nations* (Cambridge, 2004), pp. 16–19.

For the percentages of voting population in 1832, see Andrzej Walicki, *The Enlightenment and the Birth of Modern Nationhood* (Notre Dame, 1989), p. 6.

Edward Shils, 'Center and Periphery' in *Center and Periphery* (Chicago, 1975); S. N. Eisenstadt, *Comparative Civilizations and Multiple Modernities* (Leiden, 2003).

Marc Bloch, *The Royal Touch*, tr. J. E. Anderson (London, 1973).

On the *Hermannsdenkmal*, see George L. Mosse, *The Nationalization of the Masses* (Ithaca, 1975).

For the different interpretations of the Battle of Kosovo, see Vjekoslav Perica, *Balkan Idols* (Oxford, 2002).

On disputes over self-rule in the interpretation of the American Constitution, see Steven D. Ealy, 'The Federalist Papers and the Meaning of the Constitution', *Inquiries* 4/2–3 (Winter/Spring 2004): 1–10.

On the American conception of manifest destiny, see Albert K. Weinberg, *Manifest Destiny* (Baltimore, 1935).

Chapter 6

For the war camp as the origin of ancient Israel, see Julius Wellhausen, *Israelitische und Jüdische Geschichte* (Berlin, 1905), p. 24. See also Alexander Joffe, 'The Rise of Secondary States in the Iron Age Levant', *Journal of the Economic and Social History of the Orient* 45/4 (2002): 425–67. For religion and ancient Israelite nationality, see Steven Grosby, *Biblical Ideas of Nationality: Ancient and Modern* (Winona Lake, IN, 2002).

For religion in early Japan, Joseph Kitagawa, 'The Japanese *Kokutai* (National Community): History and Myth'; Matsumae Takeshi, 'Early Kami Worship' in *The Cambridge History of Japan*, ed. Delmer Brown (Cambridge, 1993), vol. I.

For the worship of the Sinhalese 'Four Warrant Gods', see Richard Gombrich and Gananath Obeyesekere, *Buddhism Transformed: Religious Change in Sri Lanka* (Princeton, 1988).

For the Virgin Mary at Blachernae, see N. Baynes, 'The Supernatural Defenders of Constantinople' in *Byzantine Studies* (London, 1955); Averil Cameron, 'The Theotokos in Sixth-Century Constantinople', *Journal of Theological Studies*, n.s., 29 (April 1978): 79–108; and Vasiliki Limberis, *Divine Heiress: The Virgin Mary and the Creation of Christian Constantinople* (London, 1994).

For the Virgin Mary at Częstochowa, see Norman Davies, *God's Playground: A History of Poland*, vol. 1.

For the tomb of the unknown soldier and other monuments to fallen soldiers, see George Mosse, *Fallen Soldiers: Reshaping the Memory of the World Wars* (New York, 1990); Jay Winter, *Sites of Memory, Sites of Mourning* (Cambridge, 1995).

For the conceptual distinction between nation and religion, see Steven Grosby, 'Nationality and Religion' in *Understanding Nationalism*, ed. M. Guibernau and J. Hutchinson (Cambridge, 2001), pp. 97–119. For the distinction between the other-worldly axial religions of the book and the this-worldly primordial religions, see Max Weber, 'The Sociology of Religion' in *Economy and Society* (Berkeley, 1978); Karl Jaspers, *The Origin and Goal of History* (New Haven, 1953); and S. N. Eisenstadt (ed.), *The Origins and Diversity of the Axial Age Civilizations* (Albany, 1986).

For the pagan elevation of the human to the divine, see E. Bickerman, 'Die Römische Kaiserapotheose', *Archiv für Religionswissenschaft* 27 (1929): 1–34; Arnaldo Momigliano, 'How Roman Emperors Became Gods', in *On Pagans, Jews, and Christians* (Middletown, Conn., 1987).

On the Greek hero, see Arthur Darby Nock, 'The Cult of the Heroes' in *Essays on Religion and the Ancient World*, ed. Zeph Stewart (Oxford, 1972).

On the cult of the saints, see Peter Brown, *The Cult of the Saints* (Chicago, 1981).

On the cult of Louis, see Elizabeth M. Hallam, 'Philip the Fair and the Cult of Saint Louis', in *Religion and National Identity*, ed. Stewart Mews (Oxford, 1982).

For Symmachus' statement, see *Prefect and Emperor: The*

Relationes of Symmachus A. D. 384, tr. R. H. Barrow (Oxford, 1973), no. 3.

Herodotus, *The History*, tr. David Grene (Chicago, 1987), Bk. 1.172.

On pagan monotheism, see Polymnia Athanassiadi and Michael Frede, *Pagan Monotheism in Late Antiquity* (Oxford, 1999).

On Marcion, still necessary is Adolph Harnack, *History of Dogma* (London, 1894).

For a succinct overview of the relation between religion and nation in Iranian history, see Charles F. Gallagher, 'The Plateau of Particularism: Problems of Religion and Nationalism in Iran', in *Churches and States*, ed. Kalman H. Silvert (New York, 1967).

For '*asabiyya*, see the *Encyclopedia of Islam* (Brill, 1960).

On the cult of Idris and the *sharifs*, see Jamil M. Abun-Nasr, *A History of the Maghrib* (Cambridge, 1975); Abdallah Laroui, *The History of the Maghrib* (Princeton, 1977).

Chapter 7

Arthur de Gobineau, *The Inequality of the Human Races*, tr. Adrian Collins (London, 1915).

Olaus Magnus, *A Compendius History of the Goths, Swedes and Vandals* (London, 1658).

Richard Verstegan, *A Restitution of Decayed Intelligence* (Antwerp, 1605).

H. S. Chamberlain, *Foundations of the Nineteenth Century* (New York, 1968).

Heinrich von Treitschke, *Politics*, tr. Blanche Dugdale and Torben de Bille (London, 1916).

For Herder's view of the nation, see Steven Grosby, 'Herder's Theory of the Nation' in *Encyclopaedia of Nationalism*, ed. A. Leoussi (New Brunswick, 2001).

Georges Dumézil, *L'idéologie tripartite des Indo-Européens* (Brussels, 1958); also by the same author, *The Destiny of the Warrior* (Chicago, 1970) and *The Destiny of a King* (Chicago, 1973), both translated into English by Alf Hiltebeitel.

For the 'clash of civilizations', see S. Huntington, *The Clash of Civilizations and the Remaking of World Order* (New York, 1996).

For criticisms of Dumézil's argument, see Colin Renfrew, *Archaeology and Language* (Cambridge 1988); Arnaldo Momigliano, 'Georges Dumézil and the Trifunctional Approach to Roman Civilization' in *On Pagans, Jews, and Christians* (Middletown, Conn., 1987).

Thomas Hobbes, *The Leviathan*, ed. Michael Oakeshott (London, 1962).

The literature of neo-Darwinism, evolutionary biology, and cognitive psychology is extensive. Useful overviews are John Cartwright, *Evolution and Human Behavior* (Cambridge, 2000); Peter J. Wilson, *Man, the Promising Primate* (New Haven, 1980); Paul R. Ehrlich, *Human Natures* (Washington, DC, 2000); J. H. Barkow, L. Cosmides, and J. Tooby (eds.), *The Adapted Mind* (Oxford, 1992); Dan Sperber, *Explaining Culture* (Oxford, 1996).

For the statistics on self-imposed female infertility, see 'Women Graduates Find Cost of Having Children Too Great', *The Times* (London), 25 April 2003; Michael S. Rendall and Steve Smallwood, 'Higher Qualifications, First Birth Timing, and Further Childbearing in England and Wales', *Population Trends* 111 (Spring 2003): 18–26.

On the 'openness of the mind', see the literature of 'philosophical anthropology', for example Max Scheler, *Man's Place in Nature*, tr. Hans Meyerhoff (Boston, 1961); Arnold Gehlen, *Man: His Nature and Place in the World*, tr. Clare McMillan and Karl Pillemer (New York, 1988); Helmuth Plessner, *Die Frage nach der Conditio humana* (Appl, 1976); *Mit anderen Augen* (Stuttgart, 1982).

Aristotle, *The Politics*, tr. Carnes Lord (Chicago, 1984), 1252a1.

Adam Smith, *The Theory of Moral Sentiments*, ed. D. D. Raphael and A. L. Macfie (Indianapolis, 1982), p. 117.

Frank Knight, 'Economic Theory and Nationalism' in *The Ethics of Competition* (New York, 1935), pp. 325, 282.

Chapter 8

For the account of the Sirens, see Homer, *The Odyssey*, tr. Richard Lattimore (New York, 1975), Book XII, lines 39–200.

The noteworthy works on the emergence of the nation as a result of modernization are Karl W. Deutsch, *Nationalism and Social Communication* (Cambridge, 1953); John Breuilly, *Nationalism and the State* (Chicago, 1982); Ernest Gellner, *Nations and Nationalism* (Ithaca, 1983); Benedict Anderson, *Imagined Communities* (London, 1983); and Liah Greenfeld, *Nationalism: Five Roads to Modernity* (Cambridge, 1992).

For the prediction that nations would soon disappear, see E. J. Hobsbawm, *Nations and Nationalism since 1780* (Cambridge, 1990).

For an example of a socialist modifying his views on the nation, see Tom Nairn, *The Break-up of Britain* (London, 1977).

Further reading

There are many books on the subjects of nations and nationalism; and, indeed, new ones appear almost daily. As a consequence, it is difficult to draw attention to even the more important ones without overlooking a number of others worthy of careful consideration, especially covering subjects that are so controversial. Thus, in addition to the works listed in the references to each chapter, I have, in what follows, provided a brief overview of a few of the more important books on nations and nationalism.

Historical works on a particular nation are almost as old as our first written records; certainly, there are examples from antiquity such as Josephus's *The Antiquities of the Jews*. Nevertheless, one can say that the scholarly study of the nation, as a problem to be explained, began in the latter half of the 18th century with two works by Johann Gottfried von Herder, *Yet Another Philosophy of History for the Education of Mankind* (New York, 1968) and *Reflections on the Philosophy of the History of Mankind* (Chicago, 1968). For a critical evaluation of these works, see Freidrich Meinecke, *Historism* (London, 1972); and Steven Grosby, 'Herder's Theory of the Nation' in *Encyclopaedia of Nationalism*, ed. Athena S. Leoussi (New Brunswick, 2001).

Discussions of the nation appeared with greater frequency in the 19th century. Some of the more noteworthy were Johann Gottlieb Fichte, *Addresses to the German Nation* (New York, 1968); Georg Wilhelm

Friedrich Hegel, *The Philosophy of History* (New York, 1956); John Emerich Edward Dalberg-Acton, 'Nationality' in *Essays in the History of Liberty* (Indianapolis, 1986); and especially Ernest Renan, 'What is a Nation?' in *The Poetry of the Celtic Races and Other Studies* (London, 1896).

Among the many works on the nation written in the aftermath of World War I, important were Freidrich Meinecke, *Cosmopolitanism and the National State* (Princeton, 1970); Johan Huizinga, 'Patriotism and Nationalism in European History' in *Men and Ideas* (Princeton, 1984); Carlton Hayes, *Essays on Nationalism* (New York, 1926); and *The Historical Evolution of Modern Nationalism* (New York, 1931). It was during this period that works by the most prolific, until recently, writer on nationalism, Hans Kohn, began to appear.

During and immediately following World War II, attempts to understand the nation, nationalism, fascism, and the political movements for national independence resulted in numerous works. Significant contributions during this period would include Hans Kohn, *The Idea of Nationalism* (New York, 1943); *The Age of Nationalism* (New York, 1962); Frederick Hertz, *Nationality in History and Politics* (London, 1944); Louis Snyder, *The Meaning of Nationalism* (New Brunswick, 1954); Karl Deutsch, *Nationalism and Social Communication* (Cambridge, 1953); Elie Kedourie, *Nationalism* (London, 1960); *Nationalism in Asia and Africa* (New York, 1970); and Hugh Seton-Watson, *Nations and States* (London, 1977). Sophisticated analyses of nations now appeared by ancient and medieval historians, for example Frank Walbank, 'The Problem of Greek Nationality' and 'Nationality as a Factor in Roman History', in *Selected Papers* (Cambridge, 1985); Ernest Kantorowicz, 'Pro Patria Mori in Medieval Political Thought', *The American Historical Review* LVI/3 (April 1951): 472–92; Gaines Post, 'Two Notes on Nationalism in the Middle Ages', *Traditio* IX (1953): 281–320; and Joseph Strayer, 'France: The Holy Land, the Chosen People, and the Most Christian King', in *Medieval Statecraft and the Perspectives of History* (Princeton, 1971). Furthermore, during this period there appeared a number of important works on the ideology of nationalism by intellectual historians such as George Mosse, *The Crisis of German Ideology* (New York, 1964).

In the last 25 years, significant works on the nation have included John Armstrong, *Nations Before Nationalism* (Chapel Hill, 1982); Dominique Schnapper, *Community of Citizens* (New Brunswick, 1998); Adrian Hastings, *The Constitution of Nationhood* (Cambridge, 1997); Steven Grosby, *Biblical Ideas of Nationality: Ancient and Modern* (Winona Lake, 2002); John Hutchinson, *Nations as Zones of Conflict* (London, 2005). Worthy of careful attention are the books by the most prolific and thoughtful writer on this subject during this period, Anthony D. Smith, *The Ethnic Origin of Nations* (Oxford, 1986); *Nationalism and Modernism* (London, 1998); *Myths and Memories of the Nation* (Oxford, 1999); *The Nation in History* (Hanover, 2000); *Chosen Peoples* (Oxford, 2004); and *The Antiquity of Nations* (Cambridge, 2004).

Other influential, recent books would include Benedict Anderson, *Imagined Communities* (London, 1983); Ernest Gellner, *Nations and Nationalism* (Ithaca, 1983); John Breuilly, *Nationalism and the State* (Chicago, 1982); and Liah Greenfeld, *Nationalism: Five Roads to Modernity* (Cambridge, 1992). There are also numerous case studies of high quality, such as John Hutchinson, *The Dynamics of Cultural Nationalism: The Gaelic Revival and the Creation of the Irish National State* (London, 1987); and works on the relation of nations and nationalism to other human activities, such as George Mosse, *Nationalism and Sexuality* (Madison, 1985); Athena Leoussi, *Nationalism and Classicism* (New York, 1998); and to philosophy, David Miller, *On Nationality* (Oxford, 1995).

Index

Expand your collection of
VERY SHORT INTRODUCTIONS

Visit the
VERY SHORT
INTRODUCTIONS
Web site

www.oup.co.uk/vsi

➤ **Information** about all published titles

➤ News of **forthcoming books**

➤ **Extracts** from the books, including titles
not yet published

➤ **Reviews** and views

➤ **Links** to other **web sites** and main
OUP web page

➤ Information about **VSIs in translation**

➤ **Contact** the editors

➤ **Order** other **VSIs** on-line

POLITICS
A Very Short Introduction
Kenneth Minogue

In this provocative but balanced essay, Kenneth Minogue discusses the development of politics from the ancient world to the twentieth century. He prompts us to consider why political systems evolve, how politics offers both power and order in our society, whether democracy is always a good thing, and what future politics may have in the twenty-first century.

'This is a fascinating book which sketches, in a very short space, one view of the nature of politics … the reader is challenged, provoked and stimulated by Minogue's trenchant views.'

Ian Davies, *Talking Politics*

'a dazzling but unpretentious display of great scholarship and humane reflection'

Neil O'Sullivan, University of Hull

www.oup.co.uk/vsi/politics

HISTORY

A Very Short Introduction

John H. Arnold

History: A Very Short Introduction is a stimulating essay about how we understand the past. The book explores various questions provoked by our understanding of history, and examines how these questions have been answered in the past. Using examples of how historians work, the book shares the sense of excitement at discovering not only the past, but also ourselves.

'A stimulating and provocative introduction to one of collective humanity's most important quests – understanding the past and its relation to the present. A vivid mix of telling examples and clear cut analysis.'

David Lowenthal, University College London

'This is an extremely engaging book, lively, enthusiastic and highly readable, which presents some of the fundamental problems of historical writing in a lucid and accessible manner. As an invitation to the study of history it should be difficult to resist.'

Peter Burke, Emmanuel College, Cambridge

www.oup.co.uk/vsi/history

GANDHI
A Very Short Introduction
Bhikhu Parekh

Gandhi was one of the few men in history to fight simultaneously on moral, religious, political, social, economic and cultural fronts. Gandhi's life and thought has had an enormous impact both within and outside India, and he continues to be widely revered as one of the greatest moral and political leaders of the twentieth century.

In this Very Short Introduction to Gandhi's life and thought, Bhikhu Parekh outlines both Gandhi's major philosophical insights and the limitations of his thought. He looks at Gandhi's spiritual view of politics, his unique form of liberal communutarianism, and his theories of oppression, non-violent action, and active citizenship. He also considers how the success of Gandhi's principles was limited by his lack of coherent theories of evil and of state and power and how his hostility to modern civilization impeded his appreciation of its complexity.

'The golden rule is to test everything in the light of reason and experience, no matter from where it comes'

Mahatma Gandhi

www.oup.co.uk/isbn/0-19-285457-7